A
Crazy
Dictionary

Other books by Leopold Fechtner:

700 Silly Jokes in Rhyme
American Wit and Gags
5000 One-and Two-Liners
Encyclopedia of Ad-Libs
Galaxy of Funny Gags

A
Crazy
Dictionary
with
6000 Silly
Definitions

by

Leopold Fechtner

RIVERCROSS PUBLISHING, INC.
Orlando

ISBN 1-58141-029-8

Library of Congress Card Number: 98-43487

First Printing

Library of Congress Cataloging-in-Publication Data

Fechtner, Leopold, 1911–
   A crazy dictionary : with 6000 silly definitions / by Leopold
Fechtner.
      p.   cm.
   ISBN 1-58141-029-8
   1. English language—Dictionaries—Humor.   2. Vocabulary—Humor.
3. Puns and punning.   I. Title.
PN6231.W64F43   1999
423'.02'07—dc21   98-43487
                                                                         CIP

This book is dedicated
to my lovely wife Fini
for her outstanding
support and patience.

Contents:

Foreword

I'm sure there is a dictionary in every household, but they are usually dry, though interesting and informative, but never funny.

That's why I compiled this crazy dictionary, interesting, informative and FUNNY.

This book belongs in every private library, because it contains not only the usual everyday words, but also many slogans, names expressions and many hundreds of definitions and explanations never before compiled in any other dictionary.

Looking for funny definitions took extensive research. I went through literally hundreds of old magazines and monthly periodicals until I found an substantial number of witty definitions and crazy explanations.

But the main source was my own humor library, the largest private humor library in the states, containing more than 4000 humor books and funny magazines.

Though it books were carefully checked and any usable material was picked for this dictionary.

Though it took more than three ways to find and compile all this material, I enjoyed the research, the checking and the selecting.

I had lots of fun preparing this dictionary and I hope

you will be amused to find so many funny definitions you never saw before.

Leopold Fechtner
Kew Gardens, N.Y.

Silly Definitions

A:
A letter that is often written but never mailed.

AAA-AA:
A new club for people who are being driven to drink.

ABALONE:
An expression of disbelief.

ABATE:
What you put on a hook when you go fishing.

ABBREV:
The abbreviation of abbreviation.

ABBREVIATE:
To make a word shorter.

ABBREVIATION:
A word that is not an abbreviation.

ABDICATION:
Reigned out.

ABORTION:
Evading the issue.

ABRIDGED DICTIONARY:
One that always omits the word you are looking up.

ABROAD:
A place people visit when there are no wars.
A word used inside our country to describe something outside.

ABSENT-MINDED:

A person who forgets to remember or remembers to forget.

ABSORB:

To swallow up but not swallow down.

ACCIDENT:

A condition of affairs in which presence of mind is good but absence of body is better.

A happening that shouldn't happen.

An event that, five minutes after it happens, anyone can see how it could have been avoided.

Something that is often caused by the driver hugging the wrong curve.

What happens when two motorists go after the same pedestrian.

ACCIDENTAL:

The opposite of oriental.

ACCORD:

A piece of thick string.

ACCORDIAN:

A device invented by a man who couldn't decide how big the fish was that got away.

A musical instrument that teaches motorists how to fold a road map.

An instrument that works like a road map, except it makes a noise when you fold it up.

An instrument whose music comes from playing both sides against the middle.

An instrument whose music is long drawn out.

ACCOUNT:

The husband of a countess.

ACCOUNTANT:

A desk jockey.

A figurehead.

A man who is hired to figure out how you didn't make as much money as you did.

A man who is paid to make figures lie.

A man who uses your books to figure his profit.

A person who records all the mistakes management makes.

ACCRUE:
People who work on a ship.
ACHE:
A long pain.
ACIREMA:
American spelled backwards.
ACORN:
An oak in a nutshell.
ACOUSTIC:
What you play pool with.
ACQUAINTANCE:
A person whom we know well enough to borrow from, but not well enough to lend to.
ACQUIRE:
A group of singers.
ACROBAT:
A man who turns a flop into a success.
ACTOR:
A man who, if you ain't talking about him, he ain't listening.
A man who is trained to keep a large group of people from coughing.
A man who plays when he works and works when he plays.
A man who tries to be everything but himself.
A show off.
The only ham that can't be cured.
ACUTE ALCOHOLIC:
An attractive drunk.
ACUTE CARE:
What you get from an attractive nurse.
ADLIBBER:
A man who stays up all night to memorize spontaneous jokes.
ADAM:
A man nobody knows from.
ADDRESSEE:
The last person to read a postcard.
ADDUCE:
The lowest card in the deck.

15

ADMIRAL:
A general at sea.

ADOLESCENCE:
The age between pigtails and cocktails.

The age between puberty and adultery.

The age when a boy stops collecting stamps and starts playing postoffice.

The age when a child tries to bring up his parents.

The age when a girl's voice changes from No to YES.

The age when boys began to notice that girls notice boys who notice girls.

The age when children begin to question the answers.

The time when children feel that their parents should be told the facts of life.

ADOLESCENT:
A youngster who acts like a baby when you don't treat him like an adult.

A youngster who is old enough to dress himself if he could just remember where he dropped his clothes.

ADOPTION:
Parents without pains.

ADORE:
A thing with a knob.

Entrance to a house.

ADULT:
A person who has stopped growing at both ends and started growing in the middle.

ADVERTISEMENT:
A picture of a pretty girl eating, wearing or holding something that someone wants to sell.

A premium paid by the public for buying products it doesn't want.

A technique that makes you think you've longed all your life for something you've never heard before.

ADVICE:
One thing that is more blessed to give than to receive.

Something like castor oil. Easy enough to give but hard to take.

What a man gives when he gets too old to set a bad example.

What most people take for a cold.

What we ask for when we want approval.

AFFECTION:

The sudden feeling that a wife gets for her husband when she wants a new fur coat.

AFFORD:

A car people drive.

AFRAID:

Scared stiff.

AFTERMATH:

The period following algebra.

AFTER-MEAL WASHUP:

Dish appointment.

AFTERNOON:

That part of the day spent figuring how we wasted the morning.

AFTERNOON TEA:

Just giggle, gabble, gobble, git.

AGE:

The only secret a woman knows how to keep.

What most women conceal because men never act theirs.

AGENT:

A man who hates actors because they take 90% of his salary.

A pickpocket with a license.

AGGRESSIVE FELINE:

Pushy cat.

AGRICULTURIST:

A farmer with a station wagon.

AIR:

A ballon with its skin off.

AIR CONDITIONING:

An invention that keeps you cool, until you get the electric bill.

AIR CONDITIONING BILL:

Fan fare.

AIR OF SUPERIORITY:

Wise guise.

AIR TRAVEL:

Seeing less and less of more and more.

AIRLINE STEWARDESS:

A tipless waitress.

A flying waitress.

AIRMAIL STAMP:

Fly paper.

AIRPLANE:

The only place where you can't walk out on dull movie.

AIRPLANE TICKET:

Fly paper.

ALARM CLOCK:

A clock whose chief trouble is that it goes off while you're asleep.

A device that enables you to rise in the world.

A non-alcoholic eye opener.

A small mechanical device to wake up people who have no children.

Something that scares the daylights out of you.

Something that gets the most abuse when it does its duty.

Something that makes man rise and whine.

ALARMS:

What an octopus is.

ALASKA:

A state where you think of Canada as the tropics.

ALCOHOL:

A liquid that's good for preserving everything but secrets.

Main ingredient of a cocktail.

Something that can make members of the opposite sex appear more attractive than they actually are.

Stuff that makes the world go round.

The life of the party.

ALCOHOLIC:

A drinker who drinks between drinks.

ALCOHOLIC ACTOR:

Ham on Rye.

ALIBI:

A slip cover.

A reason with a bad reputation.

The legal proof that a person wasn't there where he was, and therefore couldn't do what he did.

ALIMONY:

A contraction of the word; All his money!

A coupon clipped from the bonds of matrimony.

A guaranteed annual wage.

A man's cash surrender value.

A matrimonial war debt.

A matter of wife and debt.

A one-man war debt.

A reward collected by wives for staying away from their husbands.

A single blessedness with double indemnity.

A system by which one pays for the mistake of two.

An expensive soothing syrup, prescribed by a judge for a divorcee's bleeding heart.

Bounty on the mutiny.

Disinterest, compounded annually.

Giving comfort to the enemy.

Heart-earned money.

If you don't pay it in due time you do time.

Like buying film for a camera that you have lost.

Like buying gas for another man's car.

Like buying oats for a dead horse.

Like having the TV-set on after you've fallen asleep.

No good on a cold night.

Pay-when-you-go plan.

Paying a subscription to a magazine that no longer exist.

Paying for a car after it is wrecked.

Paying for a meal after you've lost your appetite.

Payment by a man who has convictions on love.

Something that enables a woman to profit by her mistakes.

Something that enables a woman who lived unhappily married to live happily unmarried.

Taxation without representation.

The billing without the cooing.

The fee a woman charges for name dropping.

The fine levied on a man guilty of matrimony.

The high cost of leaving.

The high cost of loving.

The pay-as-you-burn plan.

Time payment for the fun you had.

ALL STAR SHOW:

Planetarium.

ALLOWANCE:

What you pay your children to live with you.

ALPHABET:

Something that has more letters than a mailbox.

The only word that contains all twenty-six letters.

ALTAR:

A place where a bachelor loses control of himself.

ALTITUDE RECORD HOLDER:

Higher flier.

AMATEUR SHOW:

Maim that tune.

AMBASSADOR:

A politician who is given a job in order to get him out of the country.

An honest man sent abroad to lie for the common-wealth.

AMBITION:

Working yourself to death in order to live better.

AMEN:

The last word.

AMERICA:

A country . .

. . full of willing people. Some willing to work and some willing to let them.

. . of big opportunities. That's why so many married men get into trouble.

. . that has the automobiles but Russia has the parking space.

. . that has the biggest standard of giving.

. . that was once a melting pot but became a pressure cooker.

. . where a man can built a three-car garage and fill it with cars he doesn't own.

.. where a man can hop into a car and drive to town to collect his unemployment check.

.. where a permanent wave is temporary and a temporary tax is permanent.

.. where a typical meal consists of pizza, chow mein and blintzes.

.. where all men are created equal. If they get married, it's their own fault.

.. where anybody can become president. Maybe that's what's the trouble with it?

.. where as soon as a man can afford a large car he buys a little one.

.. where every man does what his wife pleases.

.. where every man has a equal chance to become a failure.

.. where somebody born here is endowed with life, liberty and a big share of the national debt.

.. where everybody has the opportunity to grow up to be a tax payer.

.. where everybody raises something. Farmers raise crops, people raise children and the government raises taxes.

.. where everybody is his own boss unless he is married.

.. where everytime a bartender makes a mistake a new drink is born.

.. where everytime congress makes a joke, it's a law. And everytime when they make a law, it's a joke.

.. where in the middle of winter women buy spring clothes for summer romances with fall guys.

.. where men are free to choose their own government: blonde, brunette or redhead.

.. where one quarter is covered with forests and the rest with mortgages.

.. where people are busy polluting the air, fouling the water in rivers and burning our forests, but they are still patriotic enough to take time out to sing how they love America, the beautiful.

.. where people are divided into classes. Those who have the latest appliances and those who pay cash.

.. where people are looking for less to do, more time to do it, and more pay for not getting it done.

.. where people are made up into three classes. Those who live in California, those on the way and those who wish there were.

.. where people get paid and don't work. In Russia they work and don't get paid.

.. where people have stopped eating doughnuts. It reminds them too much of the hole the country is in.

.. where people have the biggest standard of living in the world and the best medical care. It's too bad they can't afford it.

.. where some people who live in the city want to move to the country because it's too expensive in the city, while some people who live in the country want to live in the city because it's too expensive in the country.

.. where the only man who knew all the words of the Star-Spangled Banner was Francis Scott Key.

.. where the parents obey their children.

.. where there are two classes of traveling; First Class or with children.

.. where they call a president a cabinet maker.

.. where they devote 7 days to National Pickle Week and one day to fathers.

.. where they drink coffee out of a cup. In China they drink coffee out of doors.

.. where they have a good five-cent cigar. Too bad they charge a dollar for it.

.. where they have 35 million laws trying to enforce the Ten Commandments.

.. where they lock up the juries and let the defendents go free on bail.

.. where you can buy a '98 car while still paying off a '89.

.. where you can go on the air and kid politicians and where politicians go on the air and kid people.

.. where you can have a candidate complain about poverty at a $500-a-plate dinner.

.. where you can say what you think without thinking.

.. where you pay $2 for gas, $4 for a pound of coffee and $3 for a pound of hamburger and then turn on the TV to watch The Price is Right!

.. which is becoming a country of numerology. Women won't admit their age and men won't act theirs.

AMERICA:

A land of promises, especially before election.

The land of the free with no home for the brave.

AMERICAN:

A man who ..

.. acts like a Texan when he goes to Europe.

.. after eating a typical American dinner of Chow Mein and Blintzes, has some Swiss cheese, English tea, Spanish rice, and Portuguese sardines, and after having some Pizza, goes to his Volkswagen to drove to another town to see a French movie.

.. after emptying an ashtray may manage to look as if he's just finished house cleaning.

.. always goes to the Auto Show. He likes to see what's going to knock him down next year.

.. always remembers his wife's age but forgets her birthday.

.. always remembers his wife's birthday. It's the day after she reminds him of it.

.. always starts on the 3rd to celebrate July 4th by buying a fifth.

.. always thought a yard has three feet until he started cutting the grass.

.. as soon as he can afford a Plymouth, goes and buys a Cadillac.

.. attends church three times in his life. When he is hatched, when he is matched and when he is dispatched.

.. believes in dreams until he marries one.

.. boils water to make hot tea, adds ice to make it cold, adds sugar to make it sweet and adds lemon to make it sour.

.. brings home the bacon and his wife burns it.

.. buys a chair that vibrates and a car that doesn't.

23

.. buys a lifetime supply of aspirin and uses it up in two weeks.

.. buys a trouble-free car. The trouble comes free with the car.

.. buys Italian shoes, French toilet water, Continental suits, Persian rugs, Dutch cheese, a German dachshund, Turkish cigarettes, gets an English cottage with French windows and a French poodle, and wants to be recognized as a true American.

.. calls himself a bachelor until he gets married. Then you should hear what he calls himself.

.. can always tell that kind of a time he has at a party by the look on his wife's face.

.. can say anything he pleases in his own home. His wife and children never listen anyhow.

.. celebrates July 4th by getting into his Volvo, driving to the beach on Arabian gas, rolling out his Hong Kong blanket and listening to a Sony while smoking Cuban cigars, drinking Scotch whiskey, or eating Danish pastry or Duch chocolate.

.. contented years ago to wait three or four days for a stage coach, now he complains if he misses one section of the revolving door.

.. couldn't find a parking place for his car so be bought one that was already parked.

.. demands better roads, better schools and lower taxes.

.. doesn't hesitate to bawl out the President, but always speaks softly to a traffic cop.

.. doesn't know what he wants and kills himself trying to get it.

.. doesn't mind going to work. It's the long wait till quitting time that bothers him.

.. doesn't mind spending money as long as he knows it isn't going for taxes.

.. drinks only to forget the woman who is driving him to drink.

.. drinks to forget, but the only thing he forgets is when to stop.

.. drives a bank-financed car over a bond-financed highway on credit-card gas, to open a charge-account at a department store, so he can fill his savings-and-loan-financed home with installment-purchased furniture.

.. drives a foreign car, smokes English tobacco, wears Italian clothing, eats often Chinese food or French fries and English muffins

.. drives last year's car, wears this year's clothing, and spends next year's salary.

.. first buys a home and then buys a car to get away from it.

.. gets acquainted with his neighbor by meeting him down in Florida.

.. gets lots of credit. How else could be buy a new car every year?

.. gets scared if we vote a billion dollars for education, yet he is unconcerned when he finds out we are spending 3 billion a year for cigarettes.

.. gets together with other men to talk about hard times over a $25 steak.

.. gets two vacation a year. When his boss goes to Europe and when his wife goes to Florida.

.. gives his wife her present on December 15, that way she can exchange it in time for Christmas.

.. goes into a bar for an eye-opener and comes out blind.

.. goes on vacation in a hurry to slow down.

.. goes through the change of life when his child is born. It changes his life.

.. hammers on the radiator for more steam, while dressing to go skiing.

.. had a crock pot for cooking very slow, a microwave oven for cooking fast and a stove for cooking seldom.

.. has a japanese gardener, Chinese houseboy, a French maid, and a German cook, an Irish chauffeur, a Swedish housekeeper, an American secretary and a Mexican divorce.

.. has a mobile home that doesn't move, sport clothes for work, junk food that's more expensive than real food and sweat shirts for loafing.

.. has acquired a huge vocabulary by marrying one.

25

.. has both feet on the ground and both hands up in the air.

.. has burned his fingers trying to grab the Toast of the Town.

.. has enough money to last him a lifetime, unless he buys something.

.. has enough money to pay his taxes. What he needs now is some money to live on.

.. has just bought a new house and on a clear day he can see the bank that holds the mortgage.

.. has learned to work faster, relax less, spend more and die quicker.

.. has more food to eat that any man anywhere, and more diets to keep from eating.

.. has more time-saving devices and less time that any other people in the world.

.. has never seen the Statue of Liberty or an empty parking space

.. has no trouble filing his income tax report. He only has trouble paying it.

.. has the highest standard of living. Too bad he cannot afford it.

.. has given up drinking for his wife and kidneys.

.. hopes things never get as tough as his wife's pot roast.

.. is a very careful driver, always slows down when passing a red light.

.. is a very responsible person. Everytime something goes wrong, he is responsible.

.. is deeply interested in the problem of space, especially parking and closets.

.. is in debt because he spends what his friends think he makes.

.. is in favor of long TV commercials. It's the only time he has to read the evening papers.

.. is known as a small talk expert. If there is nothing to be said he will say it.

.. is looking for home atmosphere in a hotel and hotel service at home.

.. is not afraid of hard work. He could go to sleep right beside it.

.. is now putting all his money into taxes. The only thing sure to go up.

.. is proud of his parking tickets. It proves he found a place to park.

.. is proud of his right to say what he pleases, and often wishes he had the courage to do so.

.. is the master of the house and has his wife's permission to say so.

.. is 39 around the waist, 40 around chest, 96 around the golf course, 132 around the bowling alley, seldom around the house when needed and a nuisance all the time.

.. is too proud to steal, too proud to beg and too poor to pay cash. That's why he gets credit all over.

.. is trying to overcome the rubber shortage by writing checks that bounce.

.. just wishes he could afford to live the way he is living now.

.. keeps always a stiff upper lip, his nose to the grindstone and his shoulders to the wheel.

.. keeps insisting for the latest edition of the evening papers and then only reads the comics.

.. knows exactly when to take out the garbage, as soon as his wife tells him.

.. knows his golf is improving when he hits a ball in one.

.. knows the complete lineup of all the baseball teams, but only the first line of the Star-Spangled Banner.

.. knows when and where the Pilgrims landed, but has no idea why.

.. learns arithmetic to be able to keep the baseball score.

.. likes his coffee black as the devil, hot as hell, pure as an angel and sweet as love.

.. likes his job, he only complains that the paydays are too far apart.

.. likes his job, it's the work he hates.

.. likes to eat doughnuts. It's the only food you can eat and look through to watch your hat and coat.

.. likes to eat in places where they have music. Sometimes the music helps you forget the food and sometimes the food helps you forget the music.

.. likes to relax in a tub. He enjoys it so much that sometimes he even fills it with water.

.. likes to run his home like a ship with him as the captain. Too bad he married an admiral.

.. likes work. It fascinates him, He can sit and look at it for hours.

.. lives in a topsy-turvy country where people eat upside-down cake, doors go round in circles and everybody has an inside outhouse.

.. loses his balance when his wife goes shopping.

.. never cares which side his bread is buttered on, he eats both sides.

.. never drinks coffee in the morning. It keeps him awake all day.

.. never expects to find the perfect wife. But enjoys looking for it.

.. never feels he is down and out as long as he has a tankful of gas.

.. never heard a joke he didn't like.

.. never knows what he can do until he tries to undo what he has done.

.. never was on TV but twice on Radar on the parkway.

.. orders a new car three months before it comes out and then buys his wife's Christmas presents on December 24.

.. pays so much insurance to take care of the future that he is starving to death in the present.

.. really doesn't want a cheaper car. What he wants is an expensive car for less money.

.. runs around from morning till night trying to keep his earning power up with his yearning power.

.. rushes around all day to save time which he will waste at night.

.. should be able to change diapers, plan an invasion, butcher a hog, conn a ship, design a building, write a sonnet, balance accounts, build a wall, set a bone, comfort the dying, take orders, give order, cooperate, act alone, analyse and solve problems, program a computer, cook a tasty meal, fight efficiently, and die gallantly.

.. sips Brazilian coffee from an English cup while sitting on Danish furniture after coming home in a German car from a Swedish movie and then writes to his Congressman with a Japanese ballpoint pen demanding to know why so much gold is leaving the United States.

.. sit around on his Danish furniture while eating Brazilian nuts that he brought from the store in his Japanese car and writes a letter with a German pen on English paper to complain to his Congressman about the balance of trade deficit.

.. smokes English tobacco, wears Italian shoes, often eats Chinese food or French fries and English muffins and takes a foreign car to strange places with borrowed luggage, to eat Hungarian goulash, and Irish stew.

.. spends a lot of money for a garage, and then parks his car outside.

.. spends half his money on coffee to keep awake and the other half on sleeping pills to put him to sleep.

.. spends money he doesn't have, to buy things he doesn't need, to impress people he doesn't like.

.. spends more time with his TV set than with his wife.

.. uses instant coffee to dawddle away an hour.

.. waits impatiently for an elevator on the way up to the YMCA to get exercise.

.. wants the front of the bus, the back of the church, and the middle of the road.

.. will always lose weight when his wife is dieting.

.. will always talk baseball in his office and will talk business on the golf course.

.. will cross the ocean to fight for his country but won't cross the street to vote in an election.

.. will eat French toast, Portugese sardines, Russian dressing, Swiss chocolate, but not American cheese.

.. will go anywhere but not the rear of the bus.

.. will jog ten minutes for exercise and then take the elevator up to the second floor.

29

. . will jump traffic lights to save seconds, than wait patiently for hours at the first tee.

. . will oil the lawn mower for his wife every Saturday morning before he goes out to play golf.

. . will return anything you give him except a book.

. . will spend half a day looking for his vitamin pill which should make him live longer, and then drives 90 miles an hour on wet pavement to make up for the time he lost.

. . will work hard on a farm so he can move to the city where he can make money so he can retire on a farm.

. . works himself to death to make a living.

. . works himself to death so he can buy labor-saving devices.

. . would like to call the Better Business Bureau for a better business.

. . would like to have a car that will last as long as the payments.

. . would like to have a good five-second commercial.

. . would like to have a nine-to-five coffee break.

. . would like to have a pill that will make a man enjoy raking leaves more than playing golf.

. . would like to have a power mower than can be operated from an air-conditioned room.

. . . would like to have a president who really knows what this country needs.

. . would like to have a quick-drying cement that sets before kids can walk on it.

. . would like to have a roadmap a woman driver can follow.

. . would like to have a spot remower that removes spots left by other spot removers.

. . would like to have a supermarket cart with four wheels all pointing in the same direction.

. . would like to have a vending machine that honors credit cards.

. . would like to have an ashtray that looks like one.

. . would like to have fewer people telling what this country really needs.

30

. . would like to have fewer guys and more wise men.

. . would like to have less permanent waves and more permanent wives.

. . would like to have less soiled conversation and more soil conservation.

. . would like to have more free speech that's worth listening to.

. . would like to have more whittlers and fewer chiselers.

. . yells for speed laws that will stop fast driving and then won't buy a car if it can't go 100 miles an hour.

. . yells for the government to balance their budget and then borrows five dollars till payday.

. . yells with his neighbors, fights with his employees, disagrees with the minority group, fights with his family and can't understand why the United Nations don't get along with each other.

AMERICAN BARBER:

Yankee Clipper.

AMERICAN CITY:

A place where by the time you've finished paying for your home in the suburb, the city has moved 20 miles farther out.

AMOK:

Am O.K.

AMOUNT:

Generally a small amount of anything does not amount to anything.

ANATOMY:

Something that everybody has but it looks better on a girl.

The study of heavenly bodies.

The stuff you hang your clothes on.

ANCHOR:

A ship's brake.

ANECDOTE:

A revealing account of an incident that never occured in the life of some famous person.

ANGEL:

A pedestrian who jumped too late.

A person who lives in Heaven.

ANGRY TAILOR:
Sew loser.

ANESTHETITIAN:
Gas man.

ANIMAL CRACKER:
A lion-tamer's whip.

ANNOUNCE:
One-sixteenth of a pound.

ANT:
A small insect, though always at work, still finds time to go to picnics.

ANTARCTIC:
Snowman's land.
Uncle's arctic's wife.

ANTEATER:
A picknicker.

ANTIQUE:
A fugitive from the junk yard with a price on his head.
A piece of furniture on which you have finally paid the last installment.
An object that made the roundtrip to attic.
Dear old thing.
Highbrow of junk.
Junk enough to be precious.
Something so old it is worth more than it really is.
Something too old to be anything but expensive.
Something very expensive when you try to buy it, but becomes very cheap when you try to sell it.
Something whose prices increase as the value decreases.

ANTIQUE SHOP:
A junk shop that raised its prices.
A place that has everything you don't need.
Generation gap.

ANTISOCIAL:
Tea with your mother's sister.

ANTWERP:
A tiny little bug.

APARTMENT:

A place where you start to turn off the radio and find out you have been listening to the neighbor's set.

APOLOGY:
The best way for a husband to get the last word.

APOSTROPHE:
A comma that has blown its top.

APPEAR:
Something you fish off of.

APPENDICITIS:
A modern pain costing $200 more than the old-fashioned stomach ache.

APPENDIX:
Some infernal organ.

APPETIZERS:
Little things you keep eating until you lose your appetite.

APPLE:
A fruit that keeps the doctor away unless you get the seeds in your appendix.

APPRENTICESHIP:
Hire learning.

AQUARIUM:
A flooded fish market.

ARABIA:
A land where they dance Sheik to Sheik.

ARCHAEOLOGICAL EXPEDITION:
Bone voyage.
Skull duggery.

ARCHAEOLOGIST:
Someone whose career lies in ruin.

ARCHITECT:
A man who covers his mistake with ivy.

ARM:
A thing a young man likes best around his girl.

ARMY:
The unqualified leading the unwilling to the unnecessary.

ARMY GENERAL:
Attention getter.

AROMA:

A city in Italy.

A man who likes to wander.

ARREST:

What you take when you are tired.

ARROGANCE:

A pose of the body to hide the faults of the mind.

ARSONIST:

One who heats and runs.

ART:

Oodles of droodles.

ARTERY:

The study of fine paintings.

ART GALLERY:

Hall of frames.

ARTHRITIS:

Twinges in the hinges.

ASBESTOS:

Incorrect grammar for: As Well As.

ASHTRAY:

Something you put cigarette ashes in, if the room has no floor.

ASSETS:

Baby donkeys.

ASTERISK:

The little black spot in the timetable which means the train doesn't go on the day selected.

ASTRONAUT:

A cloud hopper.

A person who is able to play golf on the moon.

A spaceman who finds a place in the sun by reaching for the moon.

A whirled traveler.

ASTRONOMER:

A man who looks at the moon when he is not in love.

A man whose business is always looking up.

A night watchman.

ASTRONOMY:

Something that's over your head.

ARTERY:

The study of fine paintings.

34

ATLAS:
Finally!

ATMOSPHERE:
What a quaint little place uses instead of air.

ATROPHY:
What every athlete longs for.
What you get when you win a tournament.

ATTACK:
A noise a clock makes.
A sharp nail.

ATTIC:
A place where you keep things you will never want until you have them thrown away.

AUCTION:
A place were someone talks real fast while selling things.
A place where you get something for nodding.

AUCTIONEER:
A man who picks out your wallet with a hammer.
A man who looks forbidden.
A man who sells nothing for something to a buyer who is looking for something for nothing.

AUGUST:
The month you can't open the bus window which you couldn't close in December.

AUTOBIOGRAPHY:
Fiction written by someone who knows the facts.
The life story of a car.

AUTOGRAPH COLLECTOR:
A big name hunter.

AUTOMAT:
A car rug.
A floor covering for automobiles.

AVAIL:
A thing women wear over their faces to make it more interesting.

AVERAGE BANK ACCOUNT:
Sinking fund.

AVERAGE MAN:
Any man who thinks he is above average.

Any man you see everywhere but in the mirror.

AVERAGE PERSON:

What we all think we are not.

AVERAGE WOMAN:

One who never knows what kind of dress she doesn't want until she buys it.

AWAKE:

What a man must be in order to make his dream come true.

AX:

Chop stick.

BAA:

A brass-railed counter where drinks are served.

Sound made by a sheep.

BAABAA:

Sound made by a two sheeps.

BAABAABAA:

Sound made by a stuttering sheep.

BABIES:

Little rivets in the bond of matrimony.

BABY:

A child loved by mother.

An alimentary canal with a loud voice on one end and no responsibility on the other.

Last year's pleasure with lungs.

Mama's little yelper.

Newly wet.

The only person who can have a toothache without having any teeth.

BABY CARRIAGE:

Last year's fun on wheels.

BABY BAIR:

Beginners look.

BABY QUADRUPLETS:

Four crying out loud.

BABY SITTER:

A teenager who behaves like a grown-up, while grown-ups behave like teenagers.

A teenagers who gets five dollars an hour to eat ten dollars worth of food.

36

A person who gets hush money.

A person you pay to watch TV while the children cry themselves to sleep.

A person you sometimes hire to join your kids watching TV.

BACHELOR:

A man who . .

. . always aims to queeze.

. . always went out on double dates in college.

. . avoids bride-eyed women.

. . believes in life, liberty and happiness of pursuit.

. . believes in wine, women and soo-long.

. . believes that one can live as cheaply as two.

. . can forget his mistakes.

. . can get into bed from either side.

. . can go fishing anytime, until he gets hooked.

. . can have a girl on his knee without having her on his hands.

. . can leave his socks and wallet lying around the house.

. . can open his wallet without turning his head.

. . can take a nap—on top of his bedspread.

. . can tell his symptoms to his doctor without having his wife interrupt.

. . can use his home phone whenever he wants.

. . can't be spouse-broken.

. . can't stand the strain of a wife.

. . cheated some woman out of a divorce.

. . comes to work every morning from a different direction.

. . doesn't get around marrying. He just gets around.

. . doesn't have to leave a party when he starts to have a good time.

. . expects to marry just as soon as he finds a girl who loves him as much as he does.

. . failed to embrace his opportunity.

. . gets tangled up with a lot of women in order to avoid getting tied down to one.

. . goes to a drive-in movie on a one-seat motorcycle.

. . has a good head on his shoulder and it's a different one every night.

. . has all his romances carried off without a hitch.

. . has lots of changes to get married, but never took the chance.

. . has a cool head and cold feet.

. . has a single thought; Staying that way.

. . has been seen everywhere with women except at the altar.

. . has faults he doesn't even know about.

. . has made up his mind, that he can't make up his mind.

. . has never come up with anything definite that a girl can put on her finger.

. . has never weakened during a weekend.

. . has no button on his shirt but no hand in his pocket either.

. . has no children to speak of.

. . has no one to blame for mistakes but himself.

. . has no one to share his trouble, but very seldom has troubles.

. . has no ties except those that need pressing.

. . has one car, two suits, three girl friends and four parking tickets.

. . has taken advantage of the fact that marriage is not compulsory.

. . has the whole closet for himself.

. . has to fix only one breakfast.

. . has to wash his own back.

. . hasn't found a girl worth giving up his phone for.

. . is a free male.

. . is a permanent temptation.

. . is a rolling stone that gathers no boss.

. . is allergic to wedding cakes.

. . is crazy to get married and knows it.

. . is foot-loose and family free.

. . is known as a dame dropper.

. . is looking for a date with no string attached.

. . is lucky in love.

. . is never miss-taken.

. . is not missing anything in life, maybe a few buttons on his shirt.

. . is smart enough not to go on a hayride with a grass widow.

. . knew when to stop.

. . knows all the ankles.

. . know how to hold a girl's hand so that she doesn't get a grip on him.

. . knows if he has a girl on the string he may wind up on a leash.

. . knows more about women that men. That's why he is a bachelor.

. . knows more than one willing girl.

. . leans toward a woman but not far enough to fall.

. . likes his girl friend just the way she is: Single!

. . looks, but does not leap.

. . makes mistakes but not in front of a preacher.

. . never chases a woman he couldn't outrun.

. . never finds out how many faults he has.

. . never knows where the next kiss is coming from.

. . never lied to his wife.

. . never makes the same mistake once.

. . never Mrs. anything.

. . never says: I'll give you a ring tomorrow.

. . plays the game of love and manages to retain his amateur standing.

. . rather has a woman on his mind than on his neck.

. . takes a girl out until she wants to get married.

. . thinks he is a thing of beauty and a boy for ever.

. . tries to avoid the issue.

. . usually has his hands full trying to loosen a girl's grip.

. . wakes up in the morning with all of the blankets.

. . wants a girl on his arm but not on his neck.

. . when a girl asks him for a diamond ring, turns stone-deaf.

. . will rather mend his socks than his ways.

. . won't take YES for an answer.

. . would rather change girls than change their names.

. . would rather cook his own goose.

. . would rather wash his own socks than dry his wife's dishes.

. . wouldn't change his quarter for a better half.

BACHELOR GIRL:
A girl who is still looking for a bachelor.

BACK-SLAPPER:
A person who hopes you'll cough up something.

BACKSEAT DRIVER:
A driver who drives a driver.
One who never runs out of gas.

BACKWARDS:
A word that is always spelled backwards.

BACTERIA:
The back of a cafeteria.

BACKYARD:
Garden of weedin'.

BAD CHINESE FOOD:
Egg Phooey Yung.

BAD INTERPRETATION:
Misleading reading.

BAGDAD:
What mother did when she met father.

BAGEL:
A doughnut with hardening of the arteries.

BAGPIPES:
A musical instrument that should be seen not heard.

BAKER:
A man who has his fingers in many pies.
A man who rolls in dough.

BALANCED BUDGET:
When money in the bank and the days in the month run out together.

BALD:
Having a beautiful head of skin.

BALDHEADED MAN:
One who has less hair to comb but more face to wash.

BALDY:
Some people who wear their hair departed in the middle.

BALLERINA:
A dancer who toes her way around.
A girl gone crazy with her feet.

BALM:

A high explosive.

BANANA SKIN:

Slipper.

BAND-AID:

A scratch pad.

Help for needy musicians.

BANJO PLAYER:

A musician who has easy picking.

BANK:

An institution where you can borrow money if you can prove you don't need it.

BANK TELLER:

A fellow who makes piles of money.

BANQUET:

An affair where a speaker first eats dinner he doesn't want and then speaks about something he doesn't understand to people who don't want to hear it.

A plate of cold chicken and peas surrounded by warm appeals for donations.

BARBECUE:

A steak out.

An incinerator with a press agent.

BARBED WIRE:

Sarcastic telegram.

BARBER:

A brilliant conversationalist who occasionally shaves and cuts hair.

A man know as a cliptomanic.

A man knows as a head gardner.

A man who gets paid to get into your hair.

A man to whom you have to take your hat off.

BARBERSHOP:

A chop shop.

A clip joint.

A place where all the work is done on the premises.

BARGAIN:

A transaction in which each party thinks he has cheated the other.

Anything that is overpriced less than it could be.

Anything you can buy at yesterday's prices.

Anything you can buy only twice it's worth.

Something you don't want, sold at a price low enough to make you want it.

Something you figure out a use for after you have bought it.

BARGAIN SALE:

Where a woman ruins one dress to buy another.

BARGAIN SHOPPER:

A woman who will buy anything she thinks the store is losing money on.

BARIUM:

What you do when CPR fails.

BARK:

Pre-bite announcement.

BARS:

A place, if you go into too many of, you may come out singing a few of, and maybe land behind some of.

A place where they have no steady customers.

A thirst-aid station.

BARTENDER:

A grogman.

A man who fills more prescriptions for glasses than an optician.

A man who introduces you to the spirit world.

A man who is quick on the jigger.

A psychiatrist who works with an apron.

A psychiatrist with a vertical patient.

A vender of headaches.

The only man at the bar who knows what he is doing.

BASE FIDDLE:

A violin with mumps.

BASEBALL:

A business that can't thrive without strikes.

A game played by eighteen men who don't need exercise, watched by thousands who do.

BASEBALL BAT:

A fly swatter.

BASEBALL FAN:

A spectator sitting 500 feet from the plate who can see better than the umpire standing five feet away.

BASEBALL PARTY:
A party where all the bags are loaded.
BASKET BALL:
A game that's own or lost by a drop in the basket.
BASSINET:
A high-class crib.
What every fisherman wants.
BATH:
What you take when you find yourself in hot water.
BATHING BEACH:
A place where women reveal their figures and conceal their ages.
BATHING BEAUTY:
A girl who has a lovely profile all the way down.
A girl who wears nothing to speak of, but plenty to talk about.
A girl worth wading for.
A sand witch.
BATH MAT:
A little rug that children like to stand beside.
BATHING SUIT:
A baiting suit.
A fragment of decency.
A garment invented so that women could go naked in clothes.
A garment that begins nowhere and ends at once.
A garment that has been cut down to see level.
Two bandannas and a worried look.
BEACH:
A place at the seashore where people talk about how rich they are in town.
A place where girls show off their baiting suits.
A place where people slap you on the back and ask you how you're peeling.
A place where women go nowadays when they have nothing to wear.
BEATNICK:
A man on the bottom looking down.
A person who drops the job but keeps the coffee break.
An artist with a beard instead of a palette.

BEAUTICIAN:
A panhandler.

BEAUTIFUL:
What every woman looks like after you had a few drinks.

BEAUTIFUL BRIDE:
One who is well-groomed at the wedding.

BEAUTY:
A girl who often runs her face into a handsome figure.

The best substitute for brains.

BEAUTY CONTEST:
Lass roundup.

BEAUTY PARLOR:
Face repairer.

Places where ladies get a face full of mud and an earful of dirt.

Place where men are rare and women well-done.

Shops that make women pretty for a day.

BED:
Something to lie about.

BED LAMP:
The latest thing out.

BEE:
An insect that gives you the hives.

Buzzy busybodies.

Hum bugs.

Things with wings and stings.

BEER:
A beverage that is used to improve the estate of pretzels.

A beverage that rises in the yeast and sets in the vest.

BEER BARON:
Malty millionaire.

BELLY LAUGHS:
A mirthquake.

BENIGN:
A year older than eight.

BEST:
Something better than better.

BEST MAN:

An usher who made good.
The one who doesn't get the bride.

BEST SELLER:
A book that usually sells better than it reads.

BET:
A wager that can be lost in more ways than won.

BETTER:
What every girl should know.

BETTING:
A system of getting nothing for something.

BIBLE:
The best seller nobody reads.

BIGAMIST:
A man who . .
. . adds one and has two to carry.
. . believes variety is the spice of wife.
. . carries a picture of his wife in his otherwise empty wallet.
. . doesn't know when he's got enough.
. . doesn't know when to leave bad enough alone.
. . got the wrong number.
. . has taken one too many.
. . leads a double wife.
. . learns too late that two rites make one wrong.
. . likes to keep two himself.
. . loves not too wisely but too well.
. . makes a second mistake before correcting the first.
. . makes the same mistake twice.
. . married a beautiful woman and a cook.
. . marries twice in a wifetime.
. . thinks the plural of spouse is spice.
. . washes twice as many dishes after meals.

BIKINI:
A bare trap.
A bathing suit for hunting and for swimming.
A fishing net used to trap men.
A grab designed to keep women cold and men warm.
What a girl wears to make her seeworthy.

BILL:
A piece of paper which brings bad news.

BILL COLLECTOR:
Backdoor pounder.
The man who doesn't forget you when you have no
  money.
The man never forgets your address.
BILL POSTER:
Outdoor paperhanger.
BILLIONAIRE:
The only man who can live like a millionaire.
BILLS:
What some people have trouble meeting but most peo-
  ple have trouble dodging.
BIRTH CONTROL:
Evasion of the issue.
BIRTHDAY:
A day a child deserves, a man observes and a woman
  preserves.
An anniversary on which a man takes a day off and a
  woman takes a year off.
BLABBERMOUTH:
A person who doesn't know what to say and then goes
  ahead and says it.
BLACK EYE:
Result of a guided muscle.
BLACKBERRIES:
A fruit that should be black but is red when green.
BLOCKHEAD:
A person who gets a sliver in his fingers when he
  scratches his head.
BLONDE:
A woman who knows what gentlemen prefer.
An established bleachhead.
BLOTTER:
An absorbing subject.
Something you look for while the ink dries.
BLUE:
How a man with a red nose seldom feels.
The only color we can feel.
BLUNDERBUSS:
Kissing the wrong girl in the dark.

BLUNT PERSON:
A person who says what she thinks without thinking.
BOARDING HOUSE:
A place where hot water comes out of the cold tap and cold water comes out of the hot tap, and nobody comes out of the bathroom.
BOASTER:
A person who, every time he opens his mouth he puts his feat in.
BOAT:
A portable island.
BOAT RACE:
Sails convention.
Sail meeting.
BONBON:
Two bons.
BONER:
A man who filets fish in a restaurant.
BOOK:
A bunch of pages put together.
Something bound to sell.
BOOKIE:
A pickpocket who allows you to use your own hands.
BOOKEEPING:
The art of not returning books borrowed.
BOOKSELLER:
The best seller of best sellers.
BOOTBLACK:
A man who always takes a shine to us.
BOOTS:
What a man wants to die in so he won't stub his toes when he kicks the bucket.
BOOZE:
The milk of amnesia.
BORE:
A person who . .
. . as guests go, you wish he would.
. . can talk long enough to put you to sleep, but loud enough to keep you awake.

. . deprives you of your privacy without providing you with company.
. . gets offended when others talk while he's interrupting.
. . has a one track mind.
. . has a supply of talk that exceeds the demand.
. . has always lots of time to spare.
. . has nothing to say but insists on saying it.
. . has nothing to say but you have to listen a long time to find out.
. . has the personality of a dial tone.
. . has to hold your lapel to hold your attention.
. . holds a cocktail glass in one hand and your lapel in the other.
. . if you ask him what time it is, will tell you how to make a watch.
. . insists upon talking about himself when you want to talk about yourself.
. . is always arriving and never leaving.
. . is always giving you twice as many details as you want to hear.
. . is always me-deep in conversation.
. . is harder to get rid of than a summer cold.
. . is here today and here tomorrow.
. . is known as the still life of the party.
. . is only dull and uninteresting until you get to know him, then he is just plain boring.
. . is very oft-spoken.
. . is well informed on subjects in which you are not interested.
. . keeps you from being lonely and makes you wish you were.
. . knows a few words but uses them at great length.
. . knows a million ways the start a conversation and none to end one.
. . knows the same stories you do.
. . lights up the room when he leaves.
. . lost the art of conversation but not the power of speech.
. . never goes without saying.
. . never opens his mouth unless he has nothing to say.

48

. . never runs out of conversation—just listeners.

. . never seems to have a previous engagement.

. . never tries to make a long story short.

. . not only holds a conversation, he strangles it.

. . says a thousand things but never says goodbye.

. . sees that your company leaves at a reasonable hour.

. . syndicates the conversation.

. . takes his time taking your time.

. . talks when you want him to listen.

. . tells every little detail.

. . thinks he is cultured because he can bore you on any
   subject.

. . uses his mouth to talk while you use yours to yawn.

. . when you ask him how he is, tells you.

. . will eat with his fingers and talk with his fork.

. . will never talk about other people, only about himself.

. . won't listen when you talk about yourself.

. . would rather change his friends then his subject.

. . whom you like better the more you see him less.

. . whose life is an open book—that you don't want to
   read.

. . whose shortcoming is his long-standing.

. . whose stories always have a happy ending. Everybody
   is happy when they end.

. . whose voice is hard to extinguish over the telephone.

. . He's so dull, he could entertain a doubt.

. . When there is nothing left to say, he is still saying it.

. . You don't know what makes him tick, but you wish it
   was a time bomb.

BOREDOM:
   Dead wait.

BORROWER:
   A person who always wants to be left a loan.

BOSS:
   A man who comes in early to see who comes in late.

   A man who will raise the roof before be will raise
   your salary.

BOTTOM:
   The end.

BOW:

49

Fiddlestick.

BOWLING:

A sport that should be right down your alley.

The second most popular indoor sport.

BOWLING ALLEY:

The only place where people bother to pick up all pins.

BOX LUNCH:

A square meal.

BOXER:

A man who always hurts the one he gloves.

A man who always puts his best fist forward.

A man who makes money hand over fist.

A man who often doesn't know which side his head is battered on.

BOXING:

A striking affair.

BOY:

A lot of dirt with noise.

A lot of noise with dirt.

A noise covered with smudges.

A person who gets his hands dirty washing his face.

BOYCOTT:

A bed in shining armor.

Teeth behind bars.

BRAGGART:

A person who everytime he opens his mouth puts his foot into it.

BRAIN:

A wonderful organ, it starts working as soon as you get up and stops the minute you reach the office.

What you look for in a girl after you've looked at everything else.

BRASS:

More than one bra.

BRAT:

A child who always displays his pest manners.

A child, who when he gets what he want, doesn't want it.

A spoiled child who is always too fresh.

BREAD:

Raw toast.

BREATH:

The best thing to take before singing.

The most useful thing in the long run.

BRIDE:

A girl who begins a new life.

A girl who covers her mistake with mayonaise.

A girl who goes from lipstick to broomstick.

A girl who is well-groomed at her wedding.

A girl who turns into a wife.

A Miss who suddenly becomes a Mrs.

BRIDEGROOM:

A man who spends a lot of money on a new suit that nobody notices.

BRIDGE:

A card game during which you usually get a wonderful poker hand.

A card game in which a good deal depends upon a good deal.

Something put on a violin to get the music across.

BRIDGE EXPERT:

One who can keep a kibitzer quiet all evening.

BROADWAY:

A place where people spend money they haven't earned, to buy things they don't need, to impress people they don't like.

BROKEN RECORD:

A slipped disk.

BROKER:

A man who runs your fortune into a shoestring.

A man who wants to tie you up in stocks and bonds.

What you become when you play the stock market.

BROOKLYN BRIDGE:

The star-strangled spanner.

BUCCANEER:

Overpaying for corn on the cob.

BUDGET:

A complete record of how to manage to spend more than you earned.

A formula for determing that you need a raise again.

A mathematical confirmation of your suspicion.

A method of going broke methodically.

A system in which the outcome of the income depends on the outgo of the upkeep.

A system of reminding yourself that you can't afford the kind of living you've become accustomed to.

A system of worrying before you spend, instead of after.

A system that enables you to pay as you go   if you don't go anywhere.

A wonderful system which helps you to learn how much you spend and how little you earn.

An attempt to live below your yearnings.

An orderly system of living beyond your means.

An orderly way of discovering you can't live on what you're earning.

Something you stay within if you go without.

Telling your money where to go instead of wondering where it went.

BUFFET DINNER:

A party given by a hostess who doesn't have enough chairs for everybody.

BUILDING SUPERINTENDENT:

A man known by the temperature he keeps.

BULL:

A cow's husband.

A fatter cow.

BULLDOZER:

A sleeping bull.

BUMBLE BEE:

A house fly with bayonet.

BUMPER CROP:

The large number of car accidents.

BUREAUCRAT:

A man who shoots the bull, passes the buck, and makes seven copies of everything.

BURGLAR:

A man who is always ready to take advantage of an opening.

BURGLAR ALARM:

The perfect gift for the man who has everything.

BURIED TREASURE:
Sleeping beauty.
BURLESQUE:
A show where there are always more girls than costumes.

A take-off.

Usually a place where the attendance drops if clothing doesn't.
BURNING CHURCH:
Holy smoke.
BUS:
A public convenience which has just gone by.

A vehicle that takes you for a ride.
BUS DRIVER:
The only man who can tell a lady where to get off.

A certified adolescent transportation specialist.
BUSINESS MAN:
A man who is bald and fat because he comes out on the top after pushing his way to the front.

A man who spends time making money and then spends money killing time.
BUSYBODY:
A person who burns a scandal at both ends.

A person who is never busier than when engaging in something that's none of his business.
BUTCHER:
A man who is always ready to pick a bone with you.

A man who makes both ends meat.

A man who's usually long on waits and short on weight.

A steak holder.

An awkward man whose hands are always in his weigh.

The only man who will admit he has no brains.

The person least likely to put on extra weight.
BUTTERFLY:
A flutterby

A worm that has wings.

A worm who won his wings.
BUTTON:
A small event that always comes off.

Something whose hole is greater than itself.

BUTTRESS:
A lady butler.
BYSTANDER:
One who is injured in a street accident.
C:
Something you can't write correctly without.
CABBAGE:
The age of a taxi.
CACTUS:
An avocado whose mother was frightened by a porcupine.
CADDY:
A little cad.
An employee who is always left holding the bag.
One of those little things that counts.
CADILLAC:
A car a doctor buys not to make house calls in.
CAFE:
A place where the public pays the proprietor for the privilege of tipping the waiters for something to eat.
CAFETERIA:
Cafe de la pay.
CAIN:
A biblical character who hated his brother as long as he was Abel.
CALENDAR:
A system which plans its work a whole year ahead and never fails to finish on time.
Something that is always up-to-date.
Something whose days are numbered from the very beginning.
The proof that our days are numbered.
CALIFORNIA:
A fine place to live, if you happen to be an orange.
A place where, when you drive less than 50 miles an hour, they consider you are double-parked.
A place where it never rains. The sun just drips perspiration.
A place where people love the climate but hate the weather.

A place where saving up for a rainy day is regarded as an insult.

A wonderful place. On a clear day when the fog lifts, you can see the smog.

CALL GIRL:
A telephone operator.

CAMEL:
A cow upside down.

CAMP:
Where parents spend $1000 for eight weeks to teach their son to make a 25-cent ashtray.

CAMPHOR:
The only thing moths don't give a damphor.

CANAPE:
A sandwich cut into 24 pieces.

CANARIES:
Blonde sparrows.

CANDIDATE:
A man who runs for office while claiming he will win in a walk.

A man who stands for what he thinks the people will fall for.

A politician who quotes from public opinion polls until he's defeated and then mumbles something about the ignorance of the masses.

CANNIBAL:
A man who gets fed up with people.

A man who loves his fellow man—with gravy.

A man who sometimes has his friends for dinner.

A man who walks into a restaurant and orders a waiter.

A people eater.

CANTALOUPE:
Her mother wants a big wedding.

Not allowed to run off and get married.

CANTEEN:
A thirst-aid kit.

CAPITAL PUNISHMENT:
The Income Tax.

CAPITALIST:
A man who continues to spend less than his income.

A man who gathers a fortune he doesn't need to leave to people who don't deserve it.
CAPSIZE:
How large is your hat?
CAR:
A convenient place to sit out a traffic jam.

A machine that can't idle unless it runs.

An invention that makes people go fast and their money faster.

The first thing that strikes a visitor in New York.

Vehicle requiring monthly payments.

What a man keeps clean and vice versa.
CAR SALESMAN:
Professional transportation consultant.
CAR SICKNESS:
What everybody gets when the payments come due.
CARBUNCLE:
Bunking into your aunt's husband with our auto.
CARDIAC:
A poker wizard.
CARDIOLOGIST FEE:
Heart earned money.
CAREER WOMAN:
A person who is more interested in the shape of her future than the future of her shape.
CAREFUL DRIVER:
A motorist on the way to court to pay a speeding ticket.

A motorist who can sneak his car out of a garage without being caught by his wife.

A motorist who just saw a driver ahead of him getting a ticket.

A motorist who slows down when passing a red light.
CARNATION:
America's national flower.

Race of people who live in cars.
CARNEGIE HALL:
A music hall where people are always in tiers.
CARPENTER:
A constant knocker.

A highpriced woodpecker.

A man who's always knocking on wood.

CARPET:

A floor-covering that is bought by the yard and worn by the foot.

A girl who makes love in a car.

CARROT JUICE:

Hare tonic.

CARTOON:

Songs you hear on the car radio.

CASANOVA:

Ladybug.

CASH:

Paying with real money.

CASHEW:

Gezundheit.

CASHIER:

A man who counts in this world.

A man who is in a paying business.

A quick change artist.

CASSEROLE:

A method used by ingenious cooks to get rid of leftovers.

CASTANET:

What a fisherman does to catch a fish.

CASTOR OIL:

Ugh nog.

CAT:

A creature that never cried over split milk.

A purring mousetrap.

CATERPILLAR:

A worm in a fur coat.

A worm with a sweater on.

An upholstered worm.

CATTLE:

Grazing beefsteaks.

CAVIAR:

An expensive bread spread.

CAVITY:

A hole in the head.

CELEBRITY:

An actor with a publicity agent.

An umployed actor.

One who works all his life in order to be well-known and then goes through backstreets wearing dark glasses to avoid being recognized.

One whose name is in everything but in the telephone book.

CELERY:

Rhubard with sound effects.

CEMETERY:

A place of last resort.

A place where dead people live.

A place where people are dying to get in.

The only place where they have a good word for you after you're down.

CENSOR:

A person who specializes in cutting remarks.

A person who sticks his no's in other people's business.

CENSUS TAKER:

A man who goes from house to house increasing the population.

CENSUS TAKER IN CHINA:

Chinese checkers.

CENT:

A chip of the old buck.

CENTRAL AMERICA:

A country where presidents expire before their teams.

CHAFING DISH:

A frying pan that goes into society.

CHAIN STORE:

A store that sells chains.

CHAIR:

One of the few things that makes an impression on a nudist.

CHAMPAGNE:

A beverage that makes you see double but feel single.

Cider with needles in it.

French Seven Up.

Imprisoned water.

Park Avenue Ginger Ale.

CHARACTER:
A jerk with personality.
What one is called if one doesn't have any.
What you have left when you have lost everything you can lose.

CHATTERBOX:
A telephone booth.
An oft-spoken person.
Any woman who talks like a revolving door.

CHAUFFEUR:
A man smart enough to drive a car and clever enough not to own one.

CHEAP:
Sound made by an inexpensive canary.

CHECK STUBS:
A convenient record of how you managed to overdraw your account.

CHECKBOOK:
Where you keep a permanent record of all your good times.

CHECKMATE:
A rich husband.

CHECKROOM:
Not a place for cashing checks.

CHEF:
A man with a big enough vocabulary to give the soup a different name everyday.

CHERRY:
What people eat in their cocktails when the doctor prescribes fruit in their diet.

CHESS:
A game always played on squares.
A scientific way of killing time.

CHESS MASTER:
Concentration champ.

CHESTNUTS:
A person who is crazy about chests.

CHICKEN:
An egg plant.

The only animal we can eat before it is born and after it's dead.

What shouldn't be counted till they're in the couple.

CHICKEN CONSOMME:

The result of passing a small chicken through hot water quickly.

CHICKEN DINNER:

Biting the pullet.

CHICKLET:

A baby chicken.

CHILD:

A thing that stands half-way between an adult and the TV set.

CHILDISH GAME:

One at which your wife beats you.

CHILDREN:

Small people who aren't permitted to act as their parents did at that age.

The little things that tell.

Unreasonable facsimiles.

CHILI CON CARNE:

A hot foot in a dish.

An internal hotfoot.

CHILI SAUCE:

Ketchup with an attitude.

CHIMNEY:

The best fire escape.

CHINESE CHECKERS:

Census takers in Chinatown.

CHINESE GIRL WATCHER:

Peking Tom.

CHINESE GORILLA:

Hong Kong King Kong.

CHIROPODIST:

A man who knows his bunions.

CHIROPRACTOR:

A doctor who bills the foot.

A doctor who gets paid for what I get slapped for.

A doctor who is called a slipped disk jockey.

A doctor who kneads patients.

A doctor who makes money hand over foot.

A doctor whose fees are all back pay.

CHISELER:

A guy who follows you into a revolving door and comes out first.

CHIVALRY:

Turning your head because you hate to see a woman standing.

CHORUS GIRL:

The only one who gets somewhere by kicking constantly.

CHRISTIAN:

A religious person who knows what church he's staying away from.

CHRISTMAS:

The time of year when. .

. . both trees and husbands get trimmed up.

. . children look forward to whole year and the parents pay for the rest of time.

. . every girl wants her past forgotten and her present remembered.

. . husbands and wives exchange sensible gifts, like ties and a fur coat.

. . mother has to separate the men from the toys.

. . neither the past nor the future is important as much as the presents.

. . November runs into December. December runs into Christmas and Christmas runs into money.

. . stores trim their windows and their customers.

. . the radio keeps you awake all night, playing *Silent Night!*

. . we get children something for their fathers to play with.

. . you buy this year's presents with next year's salary.

. . you get homesick, even when you are home.

. . you stay in to see how you came out.

. . you wish people didn't come in different sizes.

CHRISTMAS TIME:

A season of anticipation, preparation, recreation, relations, prostration and recuperation.

CHURCH REPAIRS:
Plaster of parish.
CHURCH SUPPER:
Sacred chow.
CIGAR:
A roll of tobacco leaves which you smoke shorter when you smoke it longer.
CIGARETTE LIGHTER:
A wonderful object that is matchless.
CINDER:
The first thing you catch in your eye when you are traveling.
CIRCLE:
A round straight line with a hole in the middle.
A square with all corners rounded out.
What a man gets under his eyes after making the rounds.
CITY:
Millions of people being lonesome together.
CITY PLANNER:
Blocksmith.
CIVILIZATION:
Something that improves everything but people.
The advance from shoeless toes to toeless shoes.
CLAM CHOWDER:
A thick soup full with vegetables but no clams.
COMPROMISE:
A substitute that solves nothing but takes the best out of an argument.
An arrangement whereby people who can't get what they want make sure nobody else does either.
The shortest distance between two points.
When two people get what neither of them wanted.
CONCEIT:
A form of I-strain.
CONCERT:
A performance where the conversation of people is constantly interrupted by music.
CONCERT HALL:

A large room filled by a good singer and emptied by a bad one,.

CONDUCTOR:
A man who isn't afraid to face the music.

CONE:
An ice cream you can walk with.

CONEY ISLAND:
A place where the surf is one-third water and two-thirds people

CONFERENCE:
A big business term for swapping stories in somebody's office.

A group of people who individually can do nothing, but as a group can meet and can decide that nothing can be done.

A group of people who meet to keep minutes and waste hours.

A group of people with no information, who pool their ignorance.

A meeting of some people who come together to disagree.

A meeting of the bored.

A meeting where people talk about what they should be doing.

An organized dispute.

An organized method of not doing business.

CONFESSION MAGAZINE:
A place where people write their wrongs.

CONFIDENCE:
The feeling you have just before you understand the problem.

CONGRESS:
A legislative body whose members either investigate or are investigated.

CONNECTICUT BARBER:
Yankee clipper.

CONSCIENCE:
A guiltedge knife.

Something that gets a lot of credit that belongs to cold feet.

Something that hurts when everything else feels good.

Something that no's what's wrong.

The fear of being found out.

The small inner voice that tells you that you may be audited.

The small voice that makes you tell your wife something that she will find out anyway.

The small voice that tells you not to do something after you have done it.

The small voice that tells you you're going to get caught.

The small voice that warns you that someone is watching.

The still small voice that talks to its self.

The thing that tells you that instinct is wrong.

Truth ache.

CONSULT:

To seek another's approval of a course already decided upon.

CONSULTANT:

A man who is called in at the last minute to share the blame.

CONSUMER:

A person who hits the ceiling every time the prices do.

CONTACT LENS:

Mini-monocle.

CONTRACT:

A confession of mutual doubt.

CONTROL:

What firemen get blazes under.

CONVALESCENT:

A patient who is still alive.

A person who is not well but who is better than he was when he was worse than he is now.

CONVENTION:

A place where people pass lots of resolutions but few bars.

CONVENTION OF MUMMIES:

A wrap session.

CONVICT:

The only person who likes to be stopped in the middle
of a sentence.

COOK:
A pan handler.

COOKBOOK:
A book that contains a lot of stirring chapters.

COOL:
A good thing to keep in summer.

COORDINATOR:
One who transforms unorganized confusion into regimental chaos.

One who can bring organized chaos out of regimented confusion.

COPPER:
Uniformed burglar alarm

COP'S UNIFORM:
A law suit.

CORDUROY:
A groovy fabric.

CORN:
A commodity that's sold by the bushel in the Midwest,
by the fifth in the South and by the hour in TV.

CORN ON THE COB:
The food you eat like playing on a mouth organ.

CORPORATION:
A group of persons formed for individual profit without
individual responsibility.

CO-SIGNER:
A damn fool with a fountain pen.

COSMETIC:
Crease paint.

COST OF LIVING:
Income plus 10 percent.

The difference between your net income and your
gross habit.

COUGH:
Something you can't drop with a cough drop.

COUNTER ATTRACTION:
A pretty sales girl.

COUNTERFEIT:

Home-made cash.

Home-made bread.

COUNTERFEITER:

A man who gets into trouble by following a good example.

A man who has to make good money to stay in business.

A man who makes money without advertising.

COUNTER-IRRITANT:

A woman who looks at everything and buys nothing.

COUNTER SPY:

Department store detective.

COUNTERWEIGHT:

What you do when the clerk is busy.

COUNTRY MUSIC:

Pop corn.

COURTSHIP:

The period during which a girl decides whether she can do better or not.

The short interval between lipstick and broomstick.

COVER CHARGE:

A charge that doesn't cover anything.

COW:

A female bull.

An animal that doesn't give milk; you've got to take it from her.

COW EATING GRASS:

A lawn mooer.

COWARD:

One who, in a perilous emergency, thinks with his legs.

COWHIDE:

Something that keeps the cow together.

COWS:

Grazing milk bottles.

CRANBERRY:

A cherry with an acid condition.

CRATE FULL OF DUCKS:

A box of quackers.

CRAVAT:

A $60 necktie.

CRAZY PICKLE:
A daffydill.

CREDIT:
A clever financial trick that enables us to spend what we haven't got.

A commodity that becomes better the less it is used.

CREDIT CARD:
Buy pass.

Instant debt.

What people use after they run out of money.

CREDITOR:
A man who has a better memory than the debtor.

CREPE SUZETTE:
A drunken pancake with a hot foot.

CRICK:
The sound a Japanese camera makes.

CRIMINAL:
One who gets caught.

CRITIC:
One who finds a little bad in the best things.

People who go places and boo things.

CROOK:
A business rival who has just left the room.

CROSSWORD PUZZLE:
Something a conceited person does with a fountain pen.

CROWBAR:
A drinking place for birds.

CRUISE:
A trip where most of the girls are looking for husbands and most of the husbands are looking for girls.

CRUISESHIP:
Swimming hotel.

CRUMMY HUSBAND:
One who eats crackers in bed.

CRYING CONTEST:
Bawl game.

CUBIC:
Language spoken in Cuba.

CURIOSITY:

A wick in the candle of learning.

CURVE:

The longest way between two points.

CYCLONE:

Wind exceeding the speed limit.

CYNIC:

A man who believes the world is neither round nor flat, but crooked.

A man who knows the price of everything and the value of nothing.

DACHSHUND:

A god who wags his tail by remote control.

A low-down dog.

Half a dog high by a dog and a half long.

DADDY:

The kin you love to touch.

DAFFYDILL:

A crazy mixed-up pickle.

DAIRY BOSS:

Big cheese.

DANCE FLOOR:

A mob of people surrounded by music.

DANCER:

A person who is handy with his feet.

DANCING:

Hugging set to music.

The art of pulling your foot away faster than your partner can step on it.

DANDELIONS:

Bearded daisies.

DANDRUFF:

Chips of the old block.

Personal fallout.

DAREDEVIL:

A man who stops to light a cigarette in a revolving door.

DARKROOM:

A place where many girls with a negative personality are developed.

DARLING:

A husband's maiden name.

The popular form of address used in speaking to a person of the opposite sex whose name you cannot at the moment recall.

DAWN:
The break of day after night falls.

DAY:
Interval between nights.

DAYDREAMER:
A person who goes through life having a wonderful time spending money he hasn't got.

A person who has a good foundation for building castles in the air.

DEAD DUCK:
A goose that should have gone for a gander.

DEAD LETTER OFFICE:
A husband's pocket.

DEAD RINGER:
A broken alarm clock.

DEAR:
What your wife calls you when she needs money.

DEATH:
The only cure for insomnia.

DEBATE:
That which attracts the fish.

DEBT:
Something you're hardly ever out of.

The certain outcome of an uncertain income.

What most people run in to.

DEBUTANTE:
A bareback with greenbacks.

A tomato with plenty of lettuce.

DECADE:
What they say about a bad tooth.

DECEASE:
The oceans.

DECEIT:
The chair.

DECEMBER:
The month when stores trim their windows and their customers.

69

DECK OF CARDS:
The only thing that's put on the table and cut, but never eaten.

DECODING ROOM IN THE PENTAGON:
Notecracker suite.

DEDUCE:
The wild card in a poker game.

DEEP-SEA DIVER:
A man for hire to go lower.

DEFEAT:
The lower part of debody.

DEFENDANT:
A person who should always have a lawyer unless he has a friend on the jury.

DEFENDER:
Part of a car.

DEFICIT:
Something you have got when you haven't got as much as you had when you had nothing.

DEFINITION:
A word that's not a definition.
The meaning of a meaning.

DELEGATE AT LARGE:
A public official who travels without his wife.

DELIVER:
Part of the human body.

DELTA:
A river with its mouth full of mud.

DEMOCRACY:
Where every man is free to choose his own form of government, either blonde, brunette or red-head.

DENIAL:
A river in Egypt.

DENTAL X-RAY:
A preview of coming extraction.

DENTIST:
A man who . .
. . always bores you to tears.
. . always tries to pull a fast one.

70

.. can tell a woman to shut her mouth and gets away
with it.
.. dents things.
.. finds work for his own teeth by taking out those of
others.
.. gets paid for boring you.
.. gives you pain that drives you to extraction.
.. grinds out a day's work.
.. is a bridge builder.
.. is always getting on your nerve.
.. is always looking down in the mouth.
.. is called a 2th doc.
.. lives from hand to mouth.
.. nobody wants to see more than twice a year.
.. only pulls tooth, the whole tooth and nothing but the
tooth.
.. repairs broken bridges.
.. runs a filling station.
.. thinks a tooth is stronger than a friction.
.. tickles your ivories.
.. will give you the drill of your life.
.. A doctor with pull.
DENTIST'S OFFICE:
Chamber of hollers.
Filling station.
DENTISTRY:
The profession that tells you to be true to your teeth or
they will be false to you.
DEPARTMENT STORE:
A bazaar with escalators.
A place where you see many things you can do without.
DEPRESSION:
A period when people do without the things their par-
ents never had.
A period when you can't spend money you don't have.
Good times gone bad.
DEPTH:
Height turned upside down.
DERMATOLOGY:
Itch craft.

DESERTION:
The poor man's method of divorce.
DESK:
A wastebasket with drawers.
DETAIL:
The hind end.
DETECTIVE:
A policeman in disguise.
DETECTIVE STORY:
A novel whose author gets away with murder.
DETOUR:
A wrong way to the right place.
Road open for summer driving.
Something that lengthens your mileage, diminishes your gas, and strengthens your vocabulary.
The roughest distance between two points.
DEUTSCH:
German for German.
DEVOTE:
What politicians ask for.
DEVOTED HUSBAND:
One who buys more expensive gifts for his wife then for his girl friend.
DEW:
Wet air.
DIAMOND:
A chunk of coal that stuck to its job.
A precious stone that always looks larger to its owner than to anyone else.
There is nothing harder except making the payments on one.
DIAMOND BROOCH:
The pin girls love to touch.
DIAMOND CUTTER:
One who mows the grass at the ball park.
DIAMOND RING:
Something to keep the baby quiet.
DIAPER:
A changeable seat cover.
DIARY:

Anybody's home journal.

DICTATOR:

A man who thinks he can take it, no matter to whom it belongs.

A stenographer's boss.

DICTIONARY:

A book in which one word leads to another.

A book that describes one big word with another.

A book that's bound to be useful.

A guide to the right spelling of a word which can be easily located if you know how to spell it right.

A large book used for pressing flowers.

A place where death comes before life.

A spell binder.

An excellent book that's hard to read because it changes the subject too often.

Something that always has the first and last word.

The only place where divorce comes before marriage.

The only place where happiness can always be found.

The only place where success comes before work.

DIET TALK:

Prattle of the bulge.

DIETING:

A way to make you live a little longer by starving you to death.

A light diet followed by people who are too heavy.

A period a girl stops eating sweet things so she can start hearing them.

A short period of starvation preceeding a gain of five pounds.

An all day lunch break.

An attempt to miss the bloat.

Breaking the pound barrier.

Face the ration.

Girth control.

Keeping within the feed limit.

Lunch brake.

Something that makes you gain weight more slowly.

Something to take the starch out of you.

Something you can do best by eating nothing and then walking it off.

Something to stay on to take off.

Something you went off yesterday or will start tomorrow.

The art of keeping your mouth shut at the right time, such as breakfast, lunch and dinner.

The art of letting the hips fall where they sway.

The penalty for exceeding the feed limit.

The time when the days seem longer and the meals shorter.

Triumph of mind over platter.

What a family goes on when Mom can't get her slacks on.

What a woman does when she wants her shape to come in.

What a woman does when she weighs a hundred and plenty.

What people do when they want to avoid expanses.

When you get more food caught in your teeth then you get in your stomach.

Wishful shrinking.

DIGNITY:

The only thing that can't be preserved in alcohol.

DILATE:

To live a long time.

DIME:

A coin once used for money.

A dollar with all the taxes taken out.

DIMPLE:

An inside-out bump.

DINER:

A chew-chew car.

A restaurant where you can eat dirt cheap—but who wants to eat dirt?

DINNER:

What most girls will do almost anything for except cook.

DINING ROOM:

A place where people eat while the kitchen is being
   painted.
DIPLOMA:
   A man who fixed your pipes.
DIPLOMACY:
   Telling your boss he has an open mind instead of saying
      he has a hole in his head.
   The ability to take something and act as though you
      were giving it away.
   The art of convincing a man he's a liar without actually
      telling him so.
   The art of cutting the other fellow's throat without using
      a knife.
   The art of letting someone have your way.
   The art of saying things in such a way that nobody
      knows exactly what you mean.
   To do and say the nastiest things in the nicest way.
DIPLOMAT:
   A man who . .
   . . always knows what to talk about, but doesn't always
      talk about what he knows.
   . . always remembers the birthday but never the age of
      his wife.
   . . can always make himself misunderstood.
   . . can bring home the bacon without spilling the beans.
   . . can convince his wife not to hide her nice body under
      a floor length sable.
   . . can convince his wife to show off her new coat in a
      bus rather than in a taxi.
   . . can juggle a hot potato long enough for it become a
      cold issue.
   . . can keep his shirt on while getting something off his
      chest.
   . . can look happy when he has unexpected dinner guests.
   . . can make nothing sound like something.
   . . can put his best foot forward when he doesn't have a
      leg to stand on.
   . . can put his foot down without stepping someone's
      toes.

. . can tell you go to to hell so tactfully that you look
forward to the trip.
. . comes right out and says what he thinks when he
agrees with you.
. . divides his time between running for office and running
for cover.
. . fills the air with speeches and vice versa.
. . has a straight forward way of dodging issues.
. . has a hundred ways of saying nothing but no way of
saying something.
. . has great faith in his own patience.
. . lets you do all the talking while he gets what he wants.
. . never tells a woman how nice she looks in a gown, he
tells her how nice the gown looks on her.
. . praises married life while he stays single.
. . puts his cards on the table but still has some up his
sleeve.
. . straddles an issue whenever he isn't dodging one.
. . thinks twice before saying nothing.
. . will approach every question with an open mouth.
. . will lay down your life for his country.
. . will refuse to answer any question on the grounds it
might eliminate him.
. . will stand for what he thinks people will fall for.
DISC JOKEY:
A fellow who lives on spins and needles.
DISCHARGED RECORD SPINNER:
A slipped disc jockey.
DISCLOSE:
As near as this.
DISCUSSION:
An argument that nobody is interested in.
DISH:
Something often hard to cook but easy to break.
DISHWATER:
Something that causes a wedding ring to lose its luster
and fascination.
DISILLUSIONMENT:
The feeling you get when you realize you look exactly
like your passport photo.

DISMAY:
In the spring.

DISSENTER:
The tallest guy on the basketball team.

DISTANCE:
Something that's always missing between two parked cars.

The only thing that makes some girls look good.

DISTRICT ATTORNEY:
Someone awful but lawful.

DIVA:
A woman swimmer.

DIVER:
A person who always throws himself into his work.

DIVINE:
What grapes grow on.

DIVORCE:
A pardon from the life sentence or matrimony.

Going through change of life.

Marriage on the rocks.

Proof that love will always find a way out.

The past sentence of marriage.

The proof that some people marry for love and some for money, but most for a short time.

The refuge of those who do not favor a fight to the finish.

DIVORCE COURT:
Hall of blame.

DIVORCEE:
A woman who married for better or for worse, but not for good.

A woman who thinks that the proof of the wedding is in the alimony.

A woman who will get richer by degrees.

DOCTOR:
A man familiar with many tongues.

A man who enjoys poor health.

A man who is required by law to know all about women.

A man whom you see for a regular checkup to prevent a permanent checkout.

People you stick your tongue out to.
DOG:
A man's best friend because he wags his tail instead of
his tongue.

An old puppy.

The only friend you can buy for money.
DOG KENNEL:
A barking lot.

Chock full o' Mutts.
DOGMA:
Mama dog.
DOLLAR SIGN:
An S that's been double-crossed.
DON'T:
The best advice to give a man about to marry.
DONGDING:
Sound made by a bell rung backwards.
DOOR:
An obstruction used to block doorways.

What a dog is on the wrong side of.
DOOR BELL:
Something that never asks any questions but requires
many answers.
DOORKNOB:
A thing a revolving door goes around without.
DOPE RING:
A bunch of morons standing around in circle.
DOUBLE TROUBLE:
A mother-in-law with a twin sister.
DOUGHNUT:
A man crazy about money.

Dunk food.

The only food you can eat and watch your hat and coat
at the same time.
DRAFT BOARD:
The world's largest travel agency.
DRAGOON:
A fabulous monster that breathes fire.
DRAWROF:
Forward spelled backward.

DREAM:
Something vague because you see it only when your eyes are shut.

The only time you meet a better class of people.

What some men believe in until they marry one.

DREAM HOUSE:
A house that cost twice as much as you dreamed it would.

DREAMER:
A person who hopes for success.

DRESS:
A slip cover.

DRESSING ROOM:
An undressing room.

DRESS MAKER:
A person who keeps you in stitches.

DRESS SHOP:
A wearhouse.

DRILL SERGANT:
An army dentist.

DRILL TEAM:
A couple of dentists.

DRIP:
A person you can always hear but seldom turn off.

DRIVE-IN-BANK:
A place where cars can see their real owner.

DRIVE-IN-MOVIE:
A place where old films and young couples get together.

A place where there's more action going on in the cars than on the screen.

Wall-to-wall car-petting.

DRIZZLE:
A drip going steady.

DRUGGIST:
A man who is paid for counting pills.

A man who used to sell drugs.

A man who wishes everybody ill.

A soda jerk with a diploma.

DRUGSTORE:

A department store with a prescription counter.
A place where a man can get indigestion and a remedy
for it the same time.
A telephone with a business attached.
DRUGSTORE CLERK:
A fizzician.
DRUMSTICK:
Chicken on the cob.
DRUNKARD:
A gentleman who's always drinking between drinks.
DRYDOCK:
A thirsty physician.
Non-drinking physician.
DUCK:
Chicken on snow-shoes.
DUDE:
Past tense of DO.
DULL:
What a person may be even if he has a lot of polish.
DULL DINNER PARTY:
Snore-gasboard.
DUST:
Mud with all the water squeezed out.
The only thing you can be sure of getting on your radio.
DYNAMITE:
A big firecracker.
A boomstick.
E:
The beginning of every end.
EAR:
What musicians seldom play by but an audience always
listens by.
EARLY AMERICAN FURNITURE:
A black-and-white TV set.
A plug-in radio.
EARTH:
A solid substance, much desired by the seasick.
EARTHQUAKE:
Acre shaker.
Terrain wreck.

EASTER MILLINERY:
Hatrocities.
EAVESDROPPERS:
People who get in your hear.
ECCENTRIC:
People who mind their own business.
ECHO:
Holler mockery.
No sooner said than said.
Something that never speaks until spoken to.
The only thing that can cheat a woman out of the last word.
ECONOMIST:
A man who. .
. . denies himself a necessity today to buy a luxury tomorrow.
. . has a plan to do something with somebody else's money.
. . has all the answers to last year's questions.
. . is a big noise in his place of business, but just a little squeak at home.
. . is in business to change other people's business.
. . is uncertain about the future and hazy about the present.
. . knows all the answers but doesn't understand the questions.
. . knows how to throw money he doesn't have after money he never had.
. . knows more about money than people who have it.
. . talks in millions and borrows money for car-fare to go home.
. . tells you how to spend your money without getting any fun out of it.
. . tells you that in days of rising prices a dollar saved is 80 cents lost.
. . tells you what to do with your money after you've done something else with it.
. . tells you what's wrong with the world and makes you think it's your fault.
. . when he doesn't know the answer changes to subject.

ECSTASY:

A feeling you feel when you feel you are going to feel a feeling you never felt before.

EDITOR:

A literary barber.

A man who keeps things out of the paper.

A man with a little desk and a big wastebasket.

EEL:

A snake that swims.

EERIE:

An infant's hearing organ.

EFFICIENCY:

The knack of getting someone to do the job you dislike.

EFFICIENCY EXPERT:

A man who is mart enough to tell you how to run your business but too smart to start his own.

A man who spends six years in college learning how to look busy while watching you work.

EGOIST:

A man who is his own best friend.

A man who talks about himself when you want to talk about yourself.

A man who is always me-deep in conversation.

An I-dropper.

EGOTISM:

What makes a man in a rut think he's in the groove.

EGOTIST:

A man sitting in a crowded bus flirting with a woman who is standing.

A stupid person who thinks he knows as much as you do.

EGYTIAN BONE-DOCTOR:

Cairopractor.

EIFFEL TOWER:

The Empire State Building after taxes.

8-COURSE DINNER:

A 7-layer cake and coffee.

ELBOW MACARONI:

Any macaroni you find on your elbow.

ELECTION TIME:

A time when politicians don't know whether they are coming or going.

ELECTRIC FAN:
A machine that hopes to grow up and become an airplane.

A person who is crazy about electricity.

ELECTRIC GUITAR:
Extension chord.

ELECTRIC TOASTER:
A device used for sending smoke signals.

ELECTRICIAN:
A man who wired for money.

A switch doctor.

ELECTRICITY:
A discovery to make people see things in a new light.

ELECTROCARDIOGRAH:
Ticker tape.

ELEPHANT:
An animal that works for peanuts.

ELEVATOR:
Another thing that always gives you a lift.

ELEVATOR OPERATOR:
A human yo-yo.

A man who has his ups and downs.

EMBARASSMENT:
The only thing a modern girl takes the trouble to hide.

Two eyes meeting at a keyhole.

Watching the boss do what you just told him couldn't be done.

When you order something on the menu and find out the orchestra is playing it.

EMPTINESS:
The diningroom at a honeymoon lodge at breakfast time.

ENDEAVOR:
A word whose end is at the beginning.

ENDORSE:
Opposite of outdoors.

ENGAGEMENT RING:
A learner's permit.

A tourniquet applied to the third finger of a girl's left hand to stop circulation.

ENGINE:

A thing that quits pulling when it starts knocking.

ENGLISH:

A face across the Atlantic.

A language rarely heard lately.

Our mother tongue, since father seldom gets a chance to use it.

The universal language spoken almost everywhere, but in England and Boston.

EPITAPH:

A monumental lie.

A statement that usually lies above about the one who lies beneath.

ERASER:

Corrector's time.

ESCALATOR:

An invention so popular that there's standing room only.

Stairway to the stores.

ESCORT:

A woman's arm decoration.

ESKIMOS:

People who. .

. . after a few months of work call it a day.

. . are called God's frozen people.

. . are sitting on top of the world.

. . have to undress with an icepick.

. . make pies.

. . move in the best arctic circle.

ESPANOL:

Spanish for Spanish.

ESPERANTO:

A universal language that's spoken nowhere.

ETC:

A sign used to make others believe you know more than you do.

ETERNAL:

The length of the last school day.

ETERNAL SEARCH:
Looking for the car keys.
ETERNAL TRIANGLE:
Something that babies wear.
ETIQUETTE:
Is. .
. . the ability to shut your mouth before someone else wants to.
. . the art of knowing the right way to do the wrong thing.
. . the noise you don't make when eating soup.
. . knowing which end of a match should be used for a toothpick.
. . knowing which finger to put in your mouth when you whistle for the water.
. . learning to yawn with mouth closed.
EUNUCH:
A guy cut out to be a bachelor.
One who is cut off from temptation.
EVANGELIST:
A person who believes the world needs to have its faith lifted.
EVENING GOWN:
A dress a woman wears to be seen in the best places.
A dress that is more gone than gown.
A dress that starts late and ends early.
A dress where there is always plenty of room on top.
EVENT:
He didn't stay.
EVERYTHING:
What you get when you order hash.
EXERCISE:
Work that a person likes because it isn't work.
EXCLAMATION POINT:
A period that has blown his top.
EXCURSION:
A poor man's cruise.
EXECUTIVE:
A man who. .
. . can make quick decisions and is sometimes right.

.. can take two hours for lunch without hindering production.

.. decides quickly and gets somebody else to do the job.

.. delegates all the responsibility, shifts all the blame and takes all the credit.

.. dreams up an idea, has an assistant who says it can't be done, and a secretary who does it.

.. follows his work schedule to a tee.

.. gets the credit for all the work others do.

.. goes around with a worried look on his assistant's face.

.. has an answer for everything and a solution for nothing.

.. is a big gun that hasn't been fired yet.

.. is annoying the hired help by asking them to do something.

.. knows something about everything.

.. likes the feel of a good desk under his feet.

.. makes independent decisions without being fired.

.. starts on the bottom and works everybody.

.. takes one hour on the phone to explain why he can't see you for ten minutes.

.. talks golf around the office all morning and business around the golf course all afternoon.

.. talks to visitors so others can get some work done.

.. thinks YES MEN are better than no men at all.

.. travels from his air-conditioned office in an air-conditioned car to his air-conditioned club to take a steam bath.

EXECUTIVE SHAKEUP:
Title wave.

EXPECTANT FATHER:
A guy who is about to POP.

EXPECTANT WOMAN:
Momsoon.

EXPENSE ACCOUNT:
Account deceiveables.

EXPENSES:
Income plus credit.

EXPERIENCE:
Knowing which mistake to avoid the second time.

Knowledge acquired when it's too late.
Something I thought I had until I got more of it.
Something that a wise man doesn't need and a fool doesn't heed.
Something that teaches you too many darn things we don't want to learn.
Something that teaches you that you need a lot more.
The mistake we like to remember.
The name we give our mistakes.
The only thing some people possess.
The wonderful knowledge that enables you to recognize a mistake when you make it again.
What you get while looking for something else.
What you have left after you've lost everything else.
What you have when you are too old to get a job.

EXPERT:
A man who. .
. . can take some thing you already knew and make it sound confusing.
. . cuts so many corners everybody's going around in circles.
. . has a difficulty for every solution.
. . has a good reason for guessing wrong.
. . is an expert as long as he guesses right.
. . is from out of town.
. . is just beginning to understand how little he knows about the subject.
. . is known as a small talk expert. If there's nothing to be said be will say it.
. . is seldom in doubt but often in error.
. . knows a lot about very little, and keeps on learning more and more about less and less, until he finally knows all about nothing.
. . knows all the answers if you ask the right question.
. . makes his mistakes quietly.
. . walks in his sleep so he can get this rest and exercise at the same time.

EXPLAIN:
The simplest way to serve eggs.

EXPLANATION:

Something you give your wife at 4 A.M.
EXPLORATION:
Beating around the bush.
EXPLORER:
A person who gets enough material for a lecture.
EXPORTER:
A man who used to work as a porter.
EXTENT:
Lost tent.
EXTERMINATOR:
A man who is always dressed to kill.
A man who comes once a month to feed the mice.
A man who kills for a living.
FACTS:
Anything that hasn't been proven wrong.
FAD:
Something that goes in one era and out the other.
FAILURE:
A man who is always an hour late and a dollar short.
A man who is unable to cash in on his experience.
FAIRY:
A good witch.
FAITH:
Belief without evidence in what is told by one who
    speaks without knowledge of things without par-
    allel.
The thing which enables us to enjoy our religion, form
    of government and hot dog.
FAKE CHART:
A phony graph.
FALSE HOOD:
A wig.
FALSE TEETH:
Portable molars.
FALSIES:
Hidden persauders.
The bust that money can buy.
FAMILY:
A thing most needed in a modern home.

A group of people who have the same key to the same house.

FAMILY ALBUM:

A book with strange views.

FAMILY MAN:

A man who doesn't get a chance to read the Sunday paper until Monday night.

A man who replaced the money in his wallet with pictures of the wife and children.

A man who has several mouths to feed and one big mouth to listen to.

FAMILY TREE:

Generation map.

FAN DANCER:

A nudist with a cooling system.

FANATIC:

A person who's enthusiatic about something in which you have no interest.

Anyone rooting for the wrong team.

One who redoubles his energies after he has forgotten his aim.

FARM:

A hunk of land on which, if you work hard, you'll make a fortune if you strike oil.

A portion of land entirely covered by a mortgage.

FARMER:

A man who. .

. . can make plenty of money if he sells his farm to a developer.

. . is always outstanding in his field.

. . tips his hat every time he passes a tomato.

. . works from daybreak till backbreak.

FARMING:

A growing industry.

FARMING MAGAZINE:

Breeder's Digest.

FASHION:

A style that becomes out of date as soon as adopted.

FASHION EXPERT:

A man who gets woman to pay more money for fewer clothes.

FAST DRIVER:
Car wrecker.

FAT CASHIER:
A chubby checker.

FAT MAN:
A well-rounded person.

FAT PERSON:
Overstuffed.

FATHER:
A man for whom the monthly bill tolls.
A man in the family who is nether seen nor heard.
A man who buys the frills, pays the bills and signs the wills.
A man who is wired for cash.

FATHER'S DAY:
Just like Mother's Day, only you don't need to spend as much on the presents.
The day to remember the forgotten man.
The day you get the bill for Mother's day present.

FATTY:
One who exceeds the feed limit.

FAUCET:
An appliance that does a drip tease.

FEAST:
Eat wave.
Dinner at somebody else's house.

FEB. 30:
The best day to get married.

FEMALE APE:
A monkey wench.

FEMALE SCUBA:
Lady go diva.

FENCE:
A good thing to have around the house.

FERRYBOAT:
A boat that makes everybody cross.
Another thing that is always making slips.

FESTER:

The opposite of slower.
FIB:
F.B.I. spelled wrong.
FIDDLE:
What you can't feel as fit as when you get as tight as a drum.
FIGHT ARENA:
A punch bowl.
FIGURE:
Something a girl looks good with.
FILING CABINET:
A place where you can lose anything systematically.
FILLING STATION:
Dentist's chair.
FINANCIAL GENIUS:
A man who can earn money faster than his wife can spend it.
FINGERS:
What you can count on when everything else is lost.
FIRE INSURANCE:
Singe benefit.
FIREFLY:
A creature that's all lit up and no place to go.
FIREMAN:
A man who doesn't have to be told to go to blazes.
A man who never takes his eyes off the hose.
FIREPLACE:
An office for discharging people.
An opening in the wall with a built-in device to distribute the smoke through the room.
FIREPROOF:
Being related to the boss.
FIREWORK:
Pop art.
FIRMNESS:
That admirable quality in yourself that is detestable stubbornness in others.
FIRST KISS:
Something that comes only once in a lifetime.
FISH:

91

A creature that knows all the anglers.

An animal that goes on vacation the same time fishermen do.

Something that if there weren't any, people couldn't tell big stories about little.

FISH HATCHERY:

Spawn shop.

FISHERMAN:

A man who knows where to draw the line.

FISHERMAN'S MOTTO:

Bait and see.

FISHING:

A delusion surrounded by liars in old clothes.

A reel sport.

A reelaxation.

A sport generally confined to drowning worms.

A sport played with a long pole with a worm on one end and a fool on the other.

The art of dunking worms.

FISHNET:

A lot of little holes tied together with a string.

FISSION:

A popular sport.

FIT:

More than one foot.

FIVE-O'CLOCK SHADOW:

Bristle sprout.

FJORD:

A Norwegian automobile.

FLASHLIGHT:

A case to carry dead batteries.

FLATFOOT:

A person who's feet are always in somebody else's flat.

FLATTERER:

A person who says things to your face he wouldn't say behind your back.

FLATTERY:

A gift-wrapped insult.

Applause that refreshes.

Something that makes everybody sick except those
who swallow it.

FLEAS:

Insects that have gone to the dogs.

FLIRTING:

Attention without intention.

Wishful winking.

FLOOD:

A river too big for its bridges.

FLOOR:

The only thing guaranteed to stop falling hair.

FLORIDA:

A sunny place with many shady characters.

FLORIST:

A petal pusher.

FLOUNDERING:

Fish-market cartel.

FLY PAPER:

An airplane ticket.

FOG:

Misplaced clouds.

FOLK SINGER:

A guy who sings through his nose by ear.

FOOD:

Something that adds a festive touch to any meal.

FOOTBALL REFEREE:

Down crier.

FORE:

A golf bawl.

FOREIGN CAR:

A car you pay twice as much for to feel half as comfortable in.

FORFEIT:

What most animal stand on.

FORGER:

A man who gives a check a bad name.

A man who is always ready to write a wrong.

FORT:

Something between thoid and fift.

FORTUNE COOKIE:

A girl who marries for money.

FORTUNE TELLER VICTIM:

A seer sucker.

FORTY:

The age a woman stops patting herself on her back and begins under the chin.

FORUM:

Two-um plus two-um.

FOX:

A wolf who brings candy.

FRANCAIS:

French for French.

FRANCHISE:

What French girls wink with.

FRANCIS SCOTT KEY:

The only man who ever knew all the words to *The Star-Spangled Banner.*

FRANKFURTER:

A hamburger in tights.

FRECKLES:

Sun spots.

FREE:

The most attractive word in an Ad.

FREE SPEECH:

Somebody using your phone.

FRENCH FRIED POTATO:

Something that is in your mouth a few seconds, in your stomach a few hours and on your hips the rest of your life.

FRENZY:

A tiny friend.

FRESH AIR:

The only thing you get for nothing.

FRIEND:

A man who goes around saying nice things about you behind your back.

A man who has the same enemies you have.

A man who is in your corner when you are cornered.

A man who will eventually borrow money.

A man who will forever love you in spite of your
   success.
A man with whom you dare to be yourself.
FRIGHT:
   Cooked in hot oil.
FRIGHTENED SKIN DIVER:
   Chicken of the sea.
FROG:
   An animal that sits when it stands and stands when
   it sits.
   A wet toad.
FROST:
   An old flame after the engagement is broken off.
FROWN:
   A smile turned upside down.
FROZEN HOLY WATER:
   A Popsicle.
FROZEN:
   All stiff and stuck.
FRUIT:
   Tree pastry.
FRUSTRATION:
   A blind date who turns out to be your aunt.
   A skywriter in a hurricane.
   Mixed emotion.
   Trying to find your glasses without your glasses.
FUDDY-DUDDY:
   A duddy shaped like a fud.
FULL DRESS SUIT:
   Strait jacket.
FUN:
   Something like insurance. The older you get, the more
   it costs.
FUNDRAISING BANQUET:
   Bucks lunch.
FUNERAL BILL:
   Bill of rites.
FUR COAT:
   A garment that fattens the figure and slims the
   pocket book.

Something given to woman to keep her warm and quiet.

FURNITURE:

Household goods men buy to put ashtrays on.

Just another thing women like to push around.

Something that becomes antique before it is paid for.

GAMBLER:

A man who knows that money can be lost in more ways than won.

A man who never knows where his next deal is coming from.

A man who picks his own pocket.

GAMBLING:

Getting nothing for something.

GARAGE:

A groundfloor attic.

A place for everything but the car.

GARAGE SALE:

The time when your neighbor cleans out his attic.

GARBAGE CAN:

An after-dinner pail.

GARDEN:

Junior farm.

Man's effort to improve his lot.

Root awakening.

GARDENING:

A labor that begins with daybreak and ends with backbreak.

Remedial weeding.

GARLIC:

An onion equipped for chemical warfare.

GARLIC SANDWICH:

Two pieces of bread traveling in bad company.

GARMENT BUSINESS:

A business where they have only two seasons: Good or Bad.

GAS STATION:

A place where they fill your tank and empty your wallet.

GASOLINE:

Something your son can drive your car into the garage on the last drop of.

GENEALOGIST:

A man who traces back your family as far as your money will go.

GENEALOGY:

Tracing yourself back to people better than you are.

GENERAL STORE:

A store that has everything but a General.

GENIUS:

A crackpot until he hits the jackpot.

A fellow who has the ability to avoid work by doing it right the first time.

A man who can figure out his own income tax.

A man who can make money faster than his wife can spend it.

A person who can do almost anything except make a living.

A person who can rewrap a new shirt and not have any pins left over.

Some other woman's husband.

GENTLEMAN:

A man who . .

. . helps a woman across the street even if she doesn't need help.

. . holds the door open for his wife while she carries in a load of groceries.

. . is polite to you even when he has no favor to ask.

. . leaves the lawn mower where his wife can find it easily.

. . steadies the stepladder for his wife while she paints the kitchen ceiling.

. . when his wife drops something, kicks if where she can pick it up easily.

. . will step on his cigarette so it won't burn the carpet.

GENTLEMAN FARMER:

A farmer who dresses his scarecrow in a tuxedo.

GENTLEMEN'S AGREEMENT:

A deal which neither side cares to put in writing.

GEYSER:

A hole in the ground that burns.

An upside down waterfall.

GHOST:

Something imaginary that wears a white sheet.

GIANT:

Someone who is bigger than big.

GIFT SHOP:

A place where you see all the things you hope your friends won't send you for Christmas.

GIGOLO:

A fee-male.

A well-kept man.

One who believes the world owes him a loving.

GIN:

The stuff that makes punch taste bad when you don't put any in.

GINGER ALE:

Poor man's champagne.

GIRAFFE:

A gazelle designed by a committee.

An african skyscraper.

An animal in which a little food goes a long way.

A rubberneck cow.

GIRDLE:

A device to keep an unfortunate situation from spreading.

A holdup in broad daylight.

An uncomfortable item that makes woman look comfortable.

The differences between facts and figures.

GIRL:

A young person who is always something of three things; Hungry, thirsty or both.

A person who is fanatic about fashion but is not wrapped up in it.

A person who will scream at a mouse but smile at a wolf.

A young lady with bride ideas.

A young woman whose maiden aim is to change her maiden name.

Something you look damn silly dancing without.

The opposite sex.

The skin you love to clutch.

Usually a vision in the evening and a sight in the morning.

What woman over 40 call each other.

GIRL MECHANIC:

Tool pigeon.

GIRL PUTTING ON MAKEUP:

Baiting the trap.

GIRL WATCHERS:

Peer group.

GLADIATOR:

What the cannibal said after he dined on the lady explorer.

GLAMOUR GIRL:

A sight to be held.

GLOVES:

Shoes for the hand.

Something that's neither flesh nor bone, yet has four fingers and a thumb.

The only thing you can never find in a glove department.

GNOME:

A city in Alaska.

GNU:

An animal that lives in crossword puzzles.

Unused.

GO-GETTER:

A man who must walk ten blocks to find his car.

GOBLET:

A short sailor.

GOLD DIGGER:

A girl who forgets all about the past and future and simply enjoys the present.

A girl who mines her own business.

A girl who will break dates by going out with them.

A girl with a gift of grab.

A human gimme pig.

GOLF:

A game a man plays to relax when he is too tired to mow the lawn.

A game consisting of a long walk punctured with disappointments.

A game for men who are too old for girls but still want to get into a trap.

A game in which a small ball is chased by men who are too tired to chase anything else.

A game in which most of us stand too close to the ball after we hit it.

A game in which you drive hard to get to the green and then wind up in the hole.

A game that begins with a golfball and ends up with a highball.

A game that keeps you on the green, in the pink and in the red.

A game where the ball lies poorly and the players well.

Billard gone to grass.

Pool played outdoors

GOLF COURSE:

Tee plot.

GOLF DATE:

Tee for two.

GOLF SCORE:

Hole truth.

GOLFBALL:

A little round object that lies upon the ground while perspiring individuals fan it with a long stick.

An object that has to be hard hit to go anywhere.

GOLFER:

A man who hits and tells.

A man who yells FORE, takes six and puts down five.

GOOD BABY:

One that laughs half as much as it cries.

GOOD HUMOR MAN:

Sundae driver.

GOOD MORNING:

How a hospital doctor greets you.

GOOD OLD DAYS:

A time when a neighbor dropped in for a call instead
  of calling for a drop.
GOOD SPORT:
One who will always let you have your own way.
GOODBYE:
What money says when it talks.
GOSSIP:
A person who. .
. . always gets caught in her own mouth-trap.
. . always gives the benefit of the dirt.
. . always talks about things that make her speechless.
. . believes much more than she hears.
. . can give you all the details without knowing any of
    the facts.
. . can keep the secret going.
. . can't leave well enough alone.
. . carefully picks her friends—to pieces.
. . gets the best news from someone who promised to
    keep a secret.
. . has a good sense of rumor.
. . has a small vocabulary but a large turnover.
. . is a newscaster without a sponsor.
. . is always the knife of the party.
. . listens in haste and repeats in leisure.
. . puts two and two together and makes five.
. . spreads secrets.
. . suffers from a cute indiscretion.
. . tells everything she gets her ears on.
. . tells things before you have a chance to tell them.
. . turns an earful into a mouthful.
. . usually has more people to speak about then to.
. . when wound up will run somebody down.
. . would rather listen to dirt than sweep it.
A gabbag.
A molehill that becomes a mountain when someone
  adds a little dirt.
A way of saying nothing that leaves nothing unsaid.
Acid indiscretion.
An ill wind that blows no good.

Cheat-chat.

Conversation without thought.

Ear pollution.

Mouth to mouth recitation.

Mutter Inc.

Peddling meddling.

Rumortism.

Something heard over the grapevine.

Something that goes in one ear and out many mouths.

Something that's about as hard to unspread as butter.

Spice of life.

The grapevine that grows only sour grapes.

GOULASH:

The same as hash only looser.

GOURMET:

A man who likes to stay home and curl up with a good cook.

A man who never gets fed up with eating.

A man who puts salt and pepper on his toothpaste.

GOVERNOR:

A man who holds office so he can run for president.

GRADE CROSSING:

The meeting place of headlights and light heads.

GRAFFITI:

Hand writing on the wall.

GRAMMAR:

The mother of one of your parents.

GRAND CANYON:

The hole of fame.

GRANDFATHER:

a grandchild's press agent.

GRANDFATHER CLOCK:

An old-timer.

GRANDMOTHER:

A baby sitter who doesn't hang around the refrigerator.

An old lady who comes to your house, spoils the children and then goes home.

An old lady who keeps your mother from spanking you.

The forgotten baby sitter.

GRAPE:

Wine in pill form.
GRAPEFRUIT:
A low-calorie eye-wash.
An orange with an swelled head.
The only fruit that strikes back when attacked.
There is more in it than meets the eye.
GRASS FERTILIZER:
Lawn enforcement.
GRASSHOPPER:
Midget kangaroo.
GRAVY:
What you can stick your fork into no matter how tough
the meat is.
GREAT NECKERS:
Girls from Long Island.
GREEN:
What you need to paint the town red.
GREYHOUND:
A bus that stops at every hydrant.
GRIPPE:
An old-fashioned suitcase.
GROG:
A drink that often makes you feel that way.
GROOM:
A man who came along for the bride.
GROUNDHOG:
Finely chopped pork.
GRUDGE:
A place you keep your car.
GRUESOME:
Became a little larger.
GUEST TOWEL:
A small body of absorbing linen entirely surrounded by
waterproof embroidery.
Another thing that's untouched by human hands.
Something you look at but never use.
GUILLOTINE:
French chopping center.
The only guarantee for dandruff.
GUEST:

A person who comes and goes.

HAIL:

Hard-boiled drips.

Ice crispies.

HAIR:

Ear to ear carpeting.

Something on a man's head which is either parted or departed.

Something that grows on you.

HAIR DRESSER:

A person who curls up and dyes.

A person who does head work with his hand.

Bleach comber.

HAIR SPRAY:

Coif syrup.

HALLOWEEN:

The night of the witch-watch.

HALLUCINATION:

A swinging country.

HAM:

What a butcher smokes when he can't get a cigarette.

HAMBURGER:

Poor man's T-bone.

Steak that didn't pass the physical.

The last round-up.

HANGNAIL:

The usual coat hook.

HANDICAP:

Convenient hat.

HANGING:

A suspended sentence.

HANGOVER:

Something that occupies the head you didn't use last night.

The burden of too much proof.

The moaning after the night before.

When the brew of the night meets the cold of the day.

HAPPINESS:

Is. .

. . a car that starts easily.

. . a dentist who is out of town.

. . a good bank-account, a good cook and a good digestion.

. . a nightclub where the check is as small as your table.

. . a pair of warm slippers on a cold winter night.

. . a restaurant where the steaks are rare, the decor well-done and the prices medium.

. . being able to reach the spot on your back that itches.

. . being the father of a dropout from guitar school.

. . being told you don't have to take a bath tonight.

. . finding the owner of a lost bikini.

. . getting a bill you've already paid.

. . getting the last seat at the soda fountain.

. . getting up at 3 a.m. and finding two bottles. One for the baby and one for you.

. . having a husband who loves to eat in restaurants.

. . having a wife and a lighter and both are working.

. . having the finance company burn down with all the records.

. . having your little brother go off the summer camp for a week.

. . having your wife's lipstick the same color as your girl friend's.

. . helping your wife into a fur coat she bought before you were married.

. . losing a $200.00 diamond that's insured for $5,000.

. . not setting the alarm on Saturday night.

. . running out of gas in front of a bar.

. . seeing the taxi who passed you by in the rain skid into a police car.

. . signing your marriage license with disappearing ink.

. . the peculiar sensation you acquire when you are too busy to be miserable.

. . temporary situation between despair and tragedy.

. . to get called out of town on business the day your wife's relatives arrive for a visit.

. . waking up to go to work and then remembering it's Sunday.

. . watching a snow plow completely cover a parked police car.

. . watching TV at your girl's house during a power failure.

. . when you invite your in-laws for dinner and they can't make it.

. . when you speed past a state trooper's car that has a flat.

. . when your children are too old to cry and too young to borrow your car.

. . when your dentist calls to cancel your appointment.

. . when your neighbor takes 500 pictures of his vacation with the lens cap on.

. . when your phone rings after you have gotten out of the shower.

. . when your wife gets into the wrong line at the bank and makes a deposit.

. . when your wife runs away with your best friend and he comes back.

HAPPY:
What one is on vacation.

HARD LUCK:
Being shipwrecked on a desert island with your own wife.

HARD TIMES:
When all you can pay is compliments.

HARD WATER:
Ice.

HARDWARE STORE:
Tools paradise.

HARP:
A giant egg slicer.
A piano in the nude.
Grand piano after taxes.

HARPIST:
A person who pulls strings to get ahead.

HASH:
Accumulated stuff.
Food conglomerate.

HAT:
An absurd idea a woman wears on her head.
The best thing to put on a bald head.

HATCHET:
What a hen does to an egg.

HAWAII:
A place where men make passes at girls who wear grasses.

HAY:
Blond grass.

Grass a-la-mode.

Grass a la mowed.

HEAD:
A brain container.

The only thing a woman can keep under her hat.

HEAD START PROGRAM:
A father who gets up early to beat the children to the bathroom.

HEADACHE:
The best thing to take for a headache is whiskey the night before.

HEADLIGHTS:
Lamps carried on cars to blind the oncoming driver.

HEADLINES:
Wrinkles on the forehead.

HEADWAITER:
The best dressed man in the restaurant.

HEALTH:
What people drink to until they collapse.

What you lose by drinking to the other people.

HEALTH FOOD:
Food with fancy prices.

HEALTHY LAUGH:
A hardy ha-ha.

HEARTBURN:
A feeling you get when you're in love with someone.

HEAVEN:
Something that's out of this world.

HEEL:
Something that always follows a woman when she walks.

HELICOPTER:
Flying egg-beater.

HELL:
A woman alone with thousands of hats and no mirror.

HEN:
The only animal that can lay down on the job and still get results.

HEREDITY:
Something you believe in when you have a bright child.

HERMIT:
A man without a car.

HEROS:
What a man does to make a boat move.

HICCUP:
A belch you can't squelch.

A mini-burp.

HICK:
One who looks both ways before crossing a one-way street.

HI-FI SET:
Something that's easy on the ears and rough on the wallet.

HIGH:
What some people get when they take a drop.

HIGH HEELS:
Something invented by a woman who has been kissed on the forehead.

HIGH NOON:
Three martinis before lunch.

HIGHBALL:
An icecube in bad company.

HIGHBOY:
A form of greeting.

HIGHBROW:
A man who found something more interesting than women.

A person who enjoys things until they become popular.

A person who has the patience to sit through something that would make him a lowbrow if he didn't.

A person who looks at a sausage and thinks of Picasso.

HIGH-BROW OUTDOOR CONCERT:
Brahms bursting in air.

HIGHWAY:
   The space between two billboards.
   The shortest distance between two detours.
HIGHWAY ROBBERY:
   The price of a new car.
HIJACK:
   A tool for changing airplane tires.
HIKER:
   A person who walks to reduce or is reduced to walking.
HIMSELF:
   Usually the only thing that a college student gets out
      of college.
HINT:
   Something we often drop but never stop to pick up.
HIPPIE:
   A He in a Hercut.
HISTORY:
   A record of events which shouldn't have happened.
   Dry gossip.
   Gossip well told.
   Old gossip.
HIT TUNE:
   A song you can't remember but wish you could forget.
HITCHHIKER:
   Thumb fan.
HIVES:
   Eat rash.
   Something bees live in and people suffer through.
HOBBY:
   A habit that costs a lot of money.
   Getting exhausted on your own time.
   Hard work you would be ashamed to do for a living.
   Something you do to forget your worries.
   Something you go goofy over to keep from going nuts
      over things in general.
HOG CALLER:
   One who yodels to bring home the bacon.
HOG WASH:
   A pig's laundry.
HOLLAND:

A country where lovers plant tulips together.

HOLLYWOOD:

A place where:

. . everybody's trying to steal either your job or your wife.

. . if you don't succeed, a lot of people will tell you why.

. . the wedding cake outlasts the wedding.

. . they put beautiful frames in pictures.

. . they take a girl from Ohio, give her a Spanish name and send her to England to make a movie about the French revolution.

. . women reveal their anatomy and conceal their age.

. . you live happily and get married forever afterwards.

HOLLYWOOD MARRIAGE:

Much "I DO" about nothing.

HOME:

A place where . .

. . a woman puts up with her husband.

. . the landlord and the tenant are both trying to raise the rent.

. . you go when all other places are closed.

. . when certain people call, you're not.

. . you can scratch any place that itches.

. . you can take off your new shoes and put on your old manners.

. . you can trust the hash.

. . you get out of wet socks and into a dry martini.

. . you have wall-to-wall windows, wall-to-wall carpeting and wall-to-wall financing.

. . you stay while your car is being repaired.

. . you wait until your wife brings back your car.

HOME COOKING:

Is where a man thinks his wife is.

What a man misses when his wife isn't.

HOME MOVIES:

The strange view people take of things.

HOME RUN:

What you do in a ballgame when the ball goes through a window.

HONEYMOON:

A period when a man treats his wife like a new car.

A short period of doting between dating and debting.

A vacation a man takes before going to work for a new boss.

The interval between the bridal toast and burnt toast.

The thrill of a wife-time.

The time a modern couple spends in searching for a new apartment.

HORN:

The only part of an old car that doesn't make noise.

HORS D'OEURVES:

A sandwich cut up into a hundred pieces.

HORSE:

An oatsmobile.

HORSE-SENSE:

A degree of wisdom that keeps you from betting on the races.

HOSPITAL:

A place where friends of a patient go to talk to other friends of other patients.

A place where people who are run down wind up.

HOSPITAL DOCTOR:

A ward healer.

HOSPITAL VISITOR:

A person who brings flowers, candy and fruit to feed other friends who brought books and magazines.

HOSTAGE:

A lady who entertains visitors.

HOT:

What, when you burn yourself, you don't feel so.

HOT CHOCOLATE:

Stolen candy.

HOT DOG:

Man's best friend because it feeds the hand that bites it.

Tube steak.

HOT WATER:

The only thing what will not freeze.

HOTEL:

A place where guests often give up good dollars for poor quarters.

HOUSE TRAILER:

111

Roaming house.

HOUSEWARMING:
A last call for wedding presents.

HOUSEWIFE:
A woman who, when it comes to housework, likes to do nothing better.

HOUSEWORK:
Something you do that nobody notices unless you don't do it.

HOWLING SUCCESS:
The baby gets picked up.

HUG:
A roundabout way of expressing affection.
Energy gone to waist.

HUMAN DYNAMO:
A man who has everything charged.

HUMILITY:
Looking ashamed while you are telling everybody how wonderful you are.

HUMORIST:
One who originates old jokes.

HUNCH:
What you call an idea that you're afraid is wrong.

HURRICANE:
A gust appearance.

HUSBAND:
A man who. .
. . can do anything his wife puts her mind to.
. . feels his pocket every time he passes a mail box.
. . gave up privileges, he never knew he had.
. . has several small mouths to feed and one big one to listen to.
. . is spouse-broken.
. . just listens when he talks to his wife on the telephone.
. . lost his liberty in pursuit of happiness.
. . made a wrong turn in lover's lane.
A bachelor whose luck finally failed him.
A grouch a woman often nurses.
A man of few words.
A person whose chief function is to pay bills.

A woman's companion and paymate.

. . Something no woman should be without.

What is left over of a sweetheart after the nerve is removed.

HUSH-MONEY:

The fee you pay a baby sitter.

HUSTLER:

A man who always does today what ought to be put off till tomorrow.

HYPHEN:

A common go-between.

HYPOCHONDRIAC:

A man who. .

. . can read his doctor's handwriting.

. . can't leave being well enough alone.

. . claims he strained his back lifting $15 worth of groceries.

. . enjoys poor health and complains when feeling better.

. . feels bad when he feels good because he's afraid he will feel worse when he feels better.

. . finding a feather in his bed he thought he had the chickenpox.

. . goes to a cocktail party and stirs his drink with a thermometer.

. . goes to a drive-in movie in an ambulance.

. . goes to medical school to study to be a patient.

. . has a sick sense.

. . has a three-room medicine chest.

. . hates to hear how well he looks.

. . insists on being buried next to a doctor.

. . is an impatient patient.

. . is happy being miserable.

. . is so afraid of germs he won't even lick a stamp.

. . is terribly unhappy when he is happy.

. . likes to speak ill of himself.

HYPOCRITE:

A man who. .

. . can't tell the truth without lying.

. . hands his paycheck to his wife with a smile on his face.

. . looks before he weeps.

. . pays his taxes with a smile.

. . says grace over a meal prepared with a can-opener.

. . says he likes doing the dishes.

ICE:

One of the few things which really is what it's cracked up to be.

Skid stuff.

The hardest thing when you are learning to iceskate.

Water scared stiff.

Water that went to sleep in the cold.

ICE-COLD BEER:

A great relief pitcher.

ICE JAM:

What Eskimos eat on their bread.

ICE WATER:

What happens when you peel onions.

ICEBERG:

An icecube that made good.

ICE CREAM:

Freezy kid stuff.

What I do if they step on my toes.

ICESKATING:

A winter sport that people learn in several sittings.

ICICLE:

A drip caught in the draft.

A stiff piece of water.

IDEAL:

My turn to shuffle.

IDEAL DIVORCE:

When the wife gets the children and the husband gets the maid.

IDEAL HUSBAND:

The guy next door.

IDEAL MAN:

The type your mother wanted to marry before you father came along and spoiled her plan.

IDEAL SUMMER RESORT:

A place where the fish bite and the mosquitoes don't.

IDEALIST:

A man who is trying to keep politics out of politics.

IDEA:
Something that never works until you do.
IDIOT:
An apprentice moron.
IDLE RUMOR:
Guest at a summer resort.
IDLENESS:
A state that can be enjoyed only when there's lots of work to do.

Nothing to do and lots of time to do it.
IGLOO:
An icicle built for two.

Domicicle.
IGNORANCE:
That which everybody has some of, only in different subjects.

What lots of people have because they don't know any better.
ILL WIND:
Something that blows most saxophones.
ILLEGAL:
A sick bird.
ILLEGAL PARKING:
Staying longer than you should in a place where you are not allowed to stay at all.
ILLEGIBILITY:
A doctor's prescription written with a post office pen on a bus.
ILLEGIBLE WRITING:
Script tease.
ILLEGITIMATE CHILD:
Sinfant.
IMAGINATION:
Something that sits up with woman when her husband comes home late.
IMPATIENCE:
Waiting for something in a hurry.
INCOME:
Something you can't live without or within.

The amount of money which always turns out to be a little less than your expenses.

IN:
The hardest thing to give.

INCOME TAX:
Fine for reckless thriving.

Instant poverty.

INCOME TAX REDUCTION:
The kindest cut of all.

INCONGRUOUS:
Where laws are made.

INDEPENDENT SALESMAN:
A man who takes orders from no one.

INDIAN GIVER:
One who does so with reservation.

INDIAN RESERVATION:
The Home of the Brave.

INDIGESTION:
The failure to adjust a square meal to a round stomach.

INDISTINCT:
A place where people put dirty dishes.

INDORSE:
Where people stay in nasty weather.

INDUSTRIALIST:
A man who used to work for a living.

INFANCY:
The changing years.

INFANT:
A disturber of peace.

A household object that gets you down in the daytime and up at night.

INFANT CARE:
Another thing that has to be learned from the bottom up.

INFANTRY:
A baby oak.

INFECTION:
Another thing that often starts from scratch.

INFLATION:

A method of cutting a dollar bill in half without damaging the paper.

A period when the money you haven't got is worth less than before.

A shot in the arm that leaves a pain in the neck.

A time that allows you to live in a more expensive neighborhood without moving.

A time when you can't afford poverty.

A time when you earn more and more of less and less.

A time when you have too much month left over at the end of the money.

A time when your pockets are full and your stomach isn't.

Something that cost $10 a few years ago and now cost $15 just to have it fixed.

Something that may be hazardous to your wealth.

The time when prices begin where they used to end.

The time when you can put $50 worth of groceries into your glove compartment.

The time when you eat three squares meals a day and pay for six.

When a quarter pound of hamburger cost six quarters.

When you earn $10 an hour and your wife spends $6 a minute in the supermarket.

INFLUENCE:

What a woman on a party line has lots of.

INK:

Opposite of outk.

INMATE:

A husband or wife who stays home.

INNOCENT BYSTANDER:

A person so simple-minded he doesn't know enough to get out of the way.

The person who always gets hurt.

INSANE ASYLUM:

An institution whose inmates are simply crazy about it.

INSANE BLANKET:

A crazy quilt.

INSOMNIA:

The best cure for talking and walking in your sleep.

The inability to sleep when it's time to get up.

What a person has when he lies awake all night for one hour.

When you can't sleep, even on the job.

INSPIRATION:

A sudden desire to get down to work.

INSURANCE:

Something that keeps a man poor all his life so he can die rich.

INTELLIGENCE TEST:

Describing a spiral staircase or an arcordian without using your hands.

INTENSE:

Where boy scouts sleep.

INTERIOR DECORATOR:

A man who does things to your house he wouldn't dream of doing in his own.

A refined house painter.

INTERACTIVE TELEVISION:

When you lose the remote control.

INTERLUDE:

The times between times.

INTERMISSION:

When everybody comes inside to rest at a college dance.

When newly weds go out for breakfast.

INTERN:

A doctor with his own ambulance.

INTERNAL REVENUE SERVICE:

The world's most successful mail-order business.

INTERVALS:

What some people work at.

INTOXICATION:

To feel sophisticated and not be able to pronounce it.

INTUITION:

A woman's ability to detect an engagement ring in a man's voice.

Feminine radar.

Insight information.

Something that enables a woman to contradict her husband before he says anything.

The strange instinct that tells a woman she is right, whether she is or not.

INVENTION:
Birth of a notion.

INVENTORY:
What some women seem to take when they shop.

INVEST:
Not in the east.

INVESTIGATOR:
A busybody on a salary.

INVITE:
How a bride is dressed.

INVOICE:
The only voice father gets in family affairs.

IOU:
A paperweight.

IOWA FARMER:
Cornographer.

I.Q.:
Eye cue.

IRONY:
Giving father a wallet for Christmas.

ISLAND:
A place where the bottom of the sea sticks up through the water.

ITALIANO:
Italian for Italian.

ITCHES:
Something that when your both hands are full your nose always.

JACK:
What Jill went up the hill for.

JAIL:
The only place where they won't raise your rent.

JALOPY:
A scrap heap with a steering wheel.

JANITOR:
A floor-flusher.

A man known by the temperature he keeps.
A man who starts on the bottom and warms up.
A man who would rather sleep than heat.
The last person to learn that there has been a drop in temperature.
JARGON:
A missing vase.
JAYWALKER:
A person who knows it doesn't pay to go straight.
JAYWALKING:
An exercise that brings on that rundown feeling.
JAZZ:
Instant noise.
JEALOUSY:
The friendship one women has for another.
JEEP:
A cocktail shaker with three speeds.
JELLO:
Jittery pudding.
JEWELRY:
What men use to make a peach cordial.
JIGSAW PUZZLE:
Piece work.
JITTERBUG:
A patron in a public restroom looking for a dime.
JOGGERS:
Sole brothers.
JOINT ACCOUNT:
An account where one person does the depositing and the other the withdrawing.
JOKE FILE:
Jest of drawers.
JOKEBOOK:
Jest seller.
JOKE:
A form of humor enjoyed by some and misunderstood by most.
A group of words arranged to tickle you where you can't scratch.
The only thing Adam would recognize if he came back.

JOLLITY:
A happy cup of Lipton's.
JOY OF MOTHERHOOD:
What a woman experiences when all the kids are in bed.
JUDGE:
A lawyer who knew a politician.
A man in a trying position.
A referee between two lawyers.
JUICY:
Did you notice?
JULY:
Didn't you tell the truth?
JUMP:
The last word in airplanes.
JUNCTION:
A place where two roads separate.
JUNK:
Anything that has outlived its usefulness.
Something you keep for years and then throw it away
    two weeks before you need it.
JUNK DEALER:
A man who is always down in the dumps.
A man who makes cash from trash.
JUNK FOOD:
Delicious food that makes dentists rich.
JUNK MAIL:
Parcel pest.
JURY:
A group of people of average ignorance.
The only thing that doesn't work right when it's fixed.
Twelve men to decide who has the better lawyer.
JUSTICE OF THE PEACE:
A person who profits from the mistakes of others.
JUVENILE DELINQUENCY:
A time when a youngster stops asking his parents
    where he came from and tells them where to go.
JUVELINE DELINQUENTS:
Minors who are a major problem.
Children acting like their parents.
Other people's children.

KANGAROO:
An animal that carries it's brood in a snood.
An animal that never needs baby sitter.
An animal who could use a pocket watch.
An animal who is left holding the bag.
A large economy size grasshopper.
A pogo stick with a pouch.

KARATE SCHOOL:
Chopping center.

KARATE SUIT:
Lunging pajamas.

KEEPSAKE:
Something given us by someone we've forgotten.

KETCHUP:
Overtake.

KIDNAP:
When a child takes a bit of shut-eye.

KIDNEY:
A child's leg joint.

KILTS:
Air-cooled pants.

KINDERGARTEN:
A place where everyday is a holler day.

KINK:
A ruler that has two feet.

KISSING:
A lip tickle.
A meeting of two lips that results in a quickening of the impulse.
A mouthful of nothing.
A popular method of spreading germs and lowering resistance.
A sound made with your mouth to show love.
Lip service.
Mouth to mouth inspiration.
Nothing divided by two.
Something a child receives free, a young man steals, and the old men buy.
Something like a rumor because it goes from mouth to mouth.

Something that brings two persons so close together they can't see anything wrong with each other.

Something that tastes like Heaven and sounds like a cow pulling her foot out of the mud.

The best way to stop a woman from talking

The most agreeable result when two people put their heads together.

The only agreeable two-face action under the sun.

The shortest distance between two.

What happens when a girl gives you some lips.

Wasted moisture.

KITCHEN:

A place where you dirty up pots and pans and wash dishes.

A place where you take food out of cans and put it on plates.

KLEENEX:

Your daily nose-paper.

Your former girl friend who has just taken a bath.

KLEPTOMANIAC:

A high-class shoplifter.

A man who can't help himself from helping himself.

KNAPSACK:

A sleeping bag.

KNICKERBOCKER:

A long name for short pants.

KNIGHT:

A man in steel clothes who rides a horse.

KNITTING:

An occupation that gives women something to think about while talking.

KNOB:

A thing to adore.

KNOWLEDGE:

Something like money. The more you have the less you need to brag about it.

KNUCKLE:

Five pennies.

KOOK:

Make a deal.

KYZYXYZYLL:
A misprint.

LABOR DAY:
A day when nobody works.

LACKADAISICAL:
To be without a daisical.

LADY LETTER CARRIER:
A female mailman.

LADIES RESTROOM:
No man's land.

LADY:
A person who is never a gentleman.
A woman who makes it easy for a man to be a gentleman.

LADY GODIVA:
A woman who put all she had on a horse.

LADY'S HANDBAG:
A portable junkyard.

LAMB STEW:
Much ado about mutton.

LAND:
A seasick person's idea of Heaven.
The dry part of the earth.

LANDLORD:
A man who aims to lease.

LAP DOG:
A hairy hot-water bottle.

LAPLANDER:
A clumsy person in a crowded bus.

LARGE FOG:
Big-a-mist.

LARYNGITIS:
Conversation peace.

LAS VEGAS:
A place where. .
. . men get chip-wrecked.
. . the dice throws people.
. . the odds are you won't get even.
. . things never take a turn to the better.
. . wheels steer people.

. . you get tan and faded at the same time.

. . you return from with a small fortune, if you go there with a large fortune.

LASSIE:

A publicity hound.

LAUGH:

A big smile that busted.

LAUGHTER:

An inexpensive way to improve your health.

LAUNCH:

A meal between breakfast and dinner.

LAUNDRY:

A place where clothes are mangled.

A place where your clothes are worn out.

LAW OF GRAVITY:

The only law that everybody observes.

LAW SUIT:

A cop's uniform.

A matter of expenses and suspenses.

Something nobody likes to have and nobody likes to lose.

LAWYER:

A man who. .

. . helps you to get what is coming to him.

. . is known as a free-loader.

. . is willing to go to court and spend your last cent to prove he is right.

. . keeps you out of jail by putting you in the poorhouse.

. . will read a 10,000 word document and calls it a brief.

. . is at his best when doing his worst.

LAZINESS:

Nothing more than the habit of resting before getting tired.

LAZY BUTCHER:

A meat loafer.

LEAKY FAUCET:

A drip tease.

LEASE:

A written document in which the big type giveth and the small type taketh away.

LECTURER:

One with his hands in your pocket, his tongue in your ear, and his faith in your patience.

LEMON:

An orange with a grouch.

LEMON SQUEEZER:

A fellow who dances with a wall flower.

LEOPARD:

A dotted lion.

A spotted lion.

LIAR:

A person who should have a good memory.

LIBERTY:

What a man exchanges for a wife.

LIBRARY:

Bookie joint.

What you have when you borrow more books than you've lent.

LICENSE NUMBER:

The best thing to take down when you are run down.

LIE DETECTOR:

Mouth trap.

LOVE:

A word made up of two vowels, to consonants, and two fools.

LIFE:

A continous process of getting used to things we hadn't expected.

A time period in which the first half is ruined by our parents and the second half by our children.

The brief, troublesome interval between birth and death.

An everlasting struggle to keep money in and teeth and hair from falling out.

LIFE OF THE PARTY:

The person who can talk louder than the radio.

LIMBURGER:

Cream cheese with secret weapons.

LINGERIE:

Gay nighties.

LINGUIST:
A man who has mastered every tongue but his wife's.

LIQUID:
What the cat uses its tongue to.

LIQUIDATE:
Cocktail party.

LIQUOR:
A liquid that makes the world go around.
A liquid that talks mighty loud when it leaves the bottle.
A liquid you have to drink because you cannot do any-
thing else with it.
Instant courage.

LIQUOR STORE:
A house of instant booze.

LISP:
To thpeak like thith.

LITTERBUG:
A sabotourist.
A strewball.

LITTLE JOKE:
A mini Ha-ha.

LITTLE LEAGUE:
Peanut batter.

LOAFER:
A man who is trying to make both weekends meet.
A man who rests before he gets tired.

LOBSTER-NEWBURG:
A dish ordered at hotels by people who usually get
beans at home.

LOCKET:
A little lock.
A lockable locker.

LOITER:
Not now.

LOLLAPALOOZA:
Someone who had lost his lollapa.

LOLLIPOP:
An all-day sucker.

LORGNETTE:
A dirty look on a stick.

A French name for a dirty look you can hold in your hand.

A sneer on a spear.

LOS ANGELES:

A suburb looking for a city.

LOSER:

A man who puts a seashell to his ear and gets a busy signal.

LOST AND FOUND DEPARTMENT:

A place where people take things they have found and can't use.

LOVE:

A condition which starts when she sinks into his arms and ends with her arms in the sink.

A heartburn.

A passing fiance.

An island of emotion entirely surrounded by expenses.

Anything that ends up in a wedding.

It often begins at a splashing waterfall and ends up over a leaky faucet.

Co-dependency.

Softening of the heartery.

Something any man can buy and any woman gets for nothing.

Something like a mushroom. You never know whether it's the real thing until it's too late.

Something that makes the world go round.

The greatest indoor sport.

The greatest thing in the world because it's all embracing.

The only game in which two can play and both lose.

The only game that isn't postponed because of darkness.

The tenth word in every telegram.

LOVER:

A man who aims to squeeze.

A man who never leaves a girl in the dark.

LUCK:

Something that enables another person to succeed where we have failed.

LUMBER JACK:
Stump collector.
LUXURY:
Anything that isn't necessarily necessary.
LUXURY ARTICLE:
A product that cost $10 to make, $20 to buy, and $30 to repair.
LUXURY RESORT:
A place where a waiter expects a $5.00 tip when he presents a $6.00 bill for serving a $2.00 bottle of beer.
LYMPH:
To limp and lisp.
MACARONI:
Air-conditioned spaghetti.
MAD MONEY:
Psychiatrist's fee.
MADAM:
Another word which is always spelled backwards.
For whom the belles toil.
MADISON:
What the doctor makes you take.
MAGIC:
Gone with the wand.
MAGGOT:
Mother has.
MAGNIFY:
To see larger.
MAID:
A sweeping beauty.
A woman who works.
MAILMAN:
A letter bug.
MAKE-UP:
Something that makes a girl look terrible when she doesn't use any.
MAN:
A person who. .
. . falls in love with a face and makes the mistake of marrying the whole girl.

. . is always looking for home atmosphere in a hotel and
hotel service at the house.

. . is the only animal who drinks when not thirsty.

. . spends most of his life looking for an ideal woman.

. . wishes he were as wise a he thinks his wife thinks he is.

MAN ABOUT TOWN:

One who is on speaking terms with the head waiter.

MAN CRAZY ABOUT MONEY:

A doughnut.

MAN LUCKY IN LOVE:

A bachelor.

MAN OF THE HOUR:

One whose wife told him to wait a minute.

MAN WIRING FOR MONEY:

Electrician.

MANDATE:

An answer to a wallflower's prayer.

The type girls pray for.

MANICURIST:

A person who always has her hands full.

A person who is always at your finger tips.

A person who makes money hand over fist.

MANUSCRIPT:

Something that is submitted in haste and returned in
leisure.

MAP:

A piece of paper to help you get lost.

MARIGOLD:

Find a rich spouse.

MARRIAGE:

A business in which a man takes his boss along on
his vacation.

A ceremony where the grocer acquires an account the
florist once had.

A gamble that can win a full house.

A hangover that lasts a lifetime.

A knot tied by a preacher and untied by a lawyer.

A lottery where you can't tear up the ticket if you lose.

A man and a woman joined in deadlock.

A mutual misunderstanding.

A proposition that ends in a sentence.

A two-way street. It gets you coming and going.

A very big dinner with the dessert at the beginning.

A very expensive way to get your laundry free.

An arrangement that often begins with a duet and turns into a duel.

An association of two people for the benefit of one.

An institution in which the woman is the helpmate and the man the inmate.

An institution no family should be without.

An institution run by women and financed by men.

An institution that starts with billing and cooing, but only the billing lasts.

An institution that turns a night owl into a homing pigeon.

Friendship that got out of hand.

Is give and take. You'd better give it to her or she'll take it anyway.

Is like a hot bath. Once you get used to it, it's not so hot.

Is like a violin. After the beautiful music is over the strings are still attached.

Is made in Heaven, but so is thunder and lightning.

Is nature's way of keeping man from fighting with strangers.

Is one business that always has a silent partner.

Love parsonified.

Oceans of emotions surrounded by expanses of expenses.

The greatest cause of divorce.

The intermission between the wedding and the divorce.

The only institution of correction in which you select your own jailer.

The splice of life.

The time when you raise three things; Kids, your voice and your blood pressure.

When a man gets hooked with his own line.

MARRIAGE BROKER:

A fight promoter.

A licensed trouble maker.

MARRIAGE COUNSELLOR:

A spat remover.
MARRIAGE LICENSE:
A hunting permit for one dear only.
Commitment paper.
Noose paper.
MARRIAGE LICENSE BUREAU:
A dear trap.
MARRIED COUPLE:
A man and a woman who go to a drive-in movie and watch the movies.
Two people who sit on a park bench to get fresh air.
MARRIED MAN:
A bachelor who has weakened.
MARRY:
What a man and a woman do with each other when they don't know what to do with themselves.
MASSAGE PARLOR:
A place where people knead people.
MASSEUR:
A man who never rubs you the wrong way.
A man who works his fingers to the bone.
MATCH:
Something that never strikes twice at any place.
MATE OF A MALE MOUSE:
A mousewife.
MATERNITY CLOTHES:
Wait jacket.
MATERNITY DRESS:
Expect-tent.
MATERNITY WARD:
Heirport.
MAYFLOWER:
A small ship on which several millions Pilgrims came to America in 1620.
MAXIMUM:
Max won't talk.
MEALTIME:
That period when kids sit down to continue eating.
MEASLES:
A disease that comes out in pimples.

132

Visible spots on the son.

MENU:

Vittle statistics.

MERMAID:

A bottomless girl in a topless bathing suit.

Not enough fish to fry and not enough woman to love.

MESSENGER BOY:

A walking delegate.

METROPOLIS:

A town with a traffic problem.

MIAMI BEACH:

A long strip of beach surrounded by money.

A place where too many pay to much for too little.

The place of mink and money.

MIDDLE AGE:

The time when. . .

. . a doctor tells you to slow down instead of a policeman.

. . a girdle pinches a woman and her husband doesn't.

. . a lot of people your age look older than you are.

. . a man has baldness, bridgework, bifocals, baywindows and bunions.

. . a man starts complaining that the cleaners are shrinking the suits.

. . a man starts to sprint and finds himself walking.

. . a night on the town is followed by two on your back.

. . a woman selects her shoes for comfort and her sweater for warmth.

. . a woman won't tell her age and a man won't act his.

. . a woman's hair turns from gray to black.

. . after painting the town red, you have to rest a week before applying the second coat.

. . all you ever exercise is caution.

. . all your phone numbers in your little book are for doctors.

. . dangerous curves become extended detours.

. . everything is either falling out, wearing out, or spreading out.

. . Father time starts catching up with Mother Nature.

. . getting ahead means staying even.

. . it is later than you think and sooner than you expect.

133

.. it take you 15 minutes to get your breath after blowing out the candles on your birthday cake.

.. it takes you half as long to get tired and twice as long to get rested.

.. the air is springy and you are not.

.. the doctor giving you a checkup is much younger than you are.

.. the girls you whistle at thinks you must be calling a dog.

.. the gleam in your eyes is from the sun hitting your bifocals.

.. the long period between I Don't Care and Medicare.

.. the only thing on your lap is a TV-dinner.

.. the only things that agree with you are those things you don't like.

.. the only time you will see 60 again is on a speed limit sign.

.. the phone rings and you hope it's not for you.

.. we age in the middle.

.. work is a lot less fun and fun is a lot more work.

.. you are grounded for several days after flying high for one night.

.. you are reduced to reducing.

.. you are suspicious of any day on which you feel unusually good. .

.. you are too old to be fired and too young to be retired.

.. you are too tired to work and too poor to quit.

.. you begin to clash with the furniture.

.. you begin to eat what's good for you and not what you like.

.. you buy a birthday cake and the baker throws in a smoke alarm for free.

.. you can do anything you used to, but not until tomorrow.

.. you chase girls only if it is downhill.

.. you do more and more for the last time and less and less for the first time.

.. you don't care where you go, as long as you are home by 9 pm.

.. you don't care where your wife goes as long as you don't have to come along.

.. you don't feel your oats as much as you feel your corn.

.. you feel bad in the morning without having fun the night before.

.. you feel fit as a fiddle but bulge like a bass.

.. you feel just as young as ever, but only once in a while.

.. you feel like the morning after and you didn't do anything the night before.

.. you feel on Friday night like you used to feel on Monday morning.

.. you feel you always get less and less for your money at the barber.

.. you find yourself using one bend-over to pick up two things.

.. you get completely exhausted wrestling with your conscience.

.. you get thin on top and fat on your bottom.

.. you get winded going up an escalator.

.. you go all out and end up all in.

.. you have to listen to your children's advice.

.. you have to mend your ways if you don't want to come apart at the seams.

.. you hate to see dust on your furniture, so you take off your glasses.

.. you hope nobody invites you for next Saturday night.

.. you look forward to a dull evening.

.. you lose a little on top and gain a little in the middle.

.. you pay more attention to the food than to the waitress.

.. you return a wink with a blink.

.. you run for a train and you just make the next one.

.. you spend more time talking to the druggist than to the barber.

.. you still chase women but can't remember why.

.. you stop having emotions and start having symptoms.

.. you think you will feel as good as ever in a few days.

.. you walk around a puddle instead of through it.

.. you wish there were some other way to start the day than getting up in the morning.

. . you would rather not have a good time than have to recover from it.

. . your stories get longer and your savings shorter.

. . your clothes no longer fit, and it's you who needs the alteration,

. . your favorite nightspot is right in front of the TV set.

. . your feet hurt even before you get out of bed.

. . your friends get so stout and bald they don't recognize you.

. . your get-up and go has got-up and gone.

. . your head is making dates your body can't keep.

. . your knees buckle but your belt doesn't.

. . your memory gets shorter, your stamina longer and your forehead higher.

. . your narrow waist and broad mind being to change places.

. . your thought turns from passion to pension.

. . your weight lifting consists of standing up.

. . your wife tells you to pull in your stomach and you already have.

MIDDLE AGE:

Ten years older than you are.

MIDDLE-AGED WOMAN:

A slipping beauty.

MIDGET NOVELIST:

A short story writer.

MILK:

Recycled grass.

MIND:

Something like a parachute. They only function when they are open,

MINIATURE RAZOR:

A little shaver.

MINIMUM:

Minnie won't talk either.

MINISKIRTS:

A bikini for street wear.

A calculated risk.

A form of attire that's a hit below the belt.

A gone gown.

A short dress followed by a long look.

MINK:

The skin girls love to touch.

What a girl gets when she skins a wolf.

MINOR OPERATION:

Coal digging.

One performed on somebody else.

MINT:

The only place that makes money without advertising.

MIRROR:

A lie detector.

Another thing that should be looked into.

What a woman looks into to be sure her hat isn't on
straight.

MISCELLANY:

That Southern gal you so admire.

MISER:

A doughnut.

A man who lives poor so he can die rich.

MISERY:

Misery is. .

. . catching your new tie in a paper cutter.

. . dropping your heavy dictionary on your turtle.

. . having a live secret and a dead telephone.

. . having a new wardrobe and nowhere to go.

. . having the chicken pox during the week the circus is
it town.

. . pinching the secretary and finding out she's the boss'
wife.

. . the inability to conceal the fact that you've had your
fourth martini.

. . when in the last inning all bases are loaded and you
strike out.

. . when it's a real hot day and there's no water in the
pool.

. . when the doctor dies from the same thing he was treat-
ing you for.

MISNOMER:

The right name for the wrong word.

MISSING:

To sing incorrectly.

MIST:
A cloud burn in slow motion.

MISTAKE:
What a lawyer gets paid for, and a doctor buries.

MISTLETOE:
A glorious opportunity.
The original booby trap.

MISTRESS:
A cutie on the Q.T.
Something like a wife only she doesn't have to do the dishes.

MIXED EMOTION:
A time when you don't know whether to throw in the towel or keep it for crying.

MOBILE HOME:
Wheel estate.

MODERN ART:
Oodles of doodles.

MODERN FATHER:
One who is wired for cash.

MODERN GIRL:
One who is afraid of nothing except a stack of dirty dishes.
One who rouges in haste and repaints at leisure.

MODERN HOME:
One that gives you half the room for twice the money.

MODERN HOUSEWIFE:
A woman who can dish it out, but can't cook it.
A woman who has everything credit can buy.
One who makes soup just like her mother used to open.

MODERN MOTHER:
One who can hold safety pin and a cigarette in her mouth at the same time.

MODERN MUSIC:
Music played so fast you can't tell what classic it was stolen from.

MODERN PAINTING:
Pop goes the easel.

MONEY:

Green paper with pictures of dead people on it.
Something that can be lost in more ways than won.
Something that doesn't grow on trees.
Something that only millionaires don't need.
Something to write home about.
Something you feel, fold and forward to Washington.
Something you need in order to buy something you
    can't afford.
Stuff you use when you can't find your credit cards.
The poor man's credit card.
The root of all evil, but it's well worth waiting for.
What a person really needs to be wealthy.
What buys things you do without because you ain't got
    any of.
What things run into and people run out of.
What you need to paint the town red.
What your neighbor always has until you try to bor-
    row some.
MONOCLE:
A leering aid.
MONOLOGUE:
A conversation between two people, like a husband and
    a wife.
MONOPOLIST:
A man who keeps an elbow on each arm of his the-
    ater seat.
MONSOON:
A hurricane that couldn't afford to go to Florida.
A typhoon that's going steady with a tornado.
MONUMENTAL LIAR:
A person who writes epitaphs.
MOON:
A skylight.
MOONLIGHT PROBLEM:
How to make her see the light when you have her in
    the dark.
MOONLIGHTER:
A man who hold two jobs so he can drive from one to
    the other in a better car.

A man who tries to burn the candle at both ends in order to make both end meet.

MOONSHINE:
If you drink enough of it, you won't see the sunshine.

MOOSE:
A cow with a hat rack.

MOP:
A dustroyer.

MORBID:
A much higher offer.

MORNING:
The part of the day that gets up too early.

MORON:
A person who is stuck for an answer when you say hello!

A person who puts on a bathing suit when he enters a car pool.

A person who wrinkles his brow reading a comic book.

Censors think girls should have.

That which in the winter, women wouldn't be so cold, if they put.

MORTAR:
A plaster for keeping bricks together by keeping them apart.

MOSQUITO:
A flying hypodermic needle.

An insect that always bites the hand that feeds him.

The original skin diver.

Things you pat on your back.

MOTEL:
A place where all the rooms except the bathroom are in the living-room.

Love-Inn.

MOTH:
A perverse creature that spends the summer in a fur coat and the winter in a bathing suit.

MOTHERHOOD:
The thrill of a wifetime.

MOTHER-IN-LAW:
A guest you never invited.

A matrimonial kin that gets under your skin.
A person who goes too far by remaining too near.
A puzzle full of crosswords.
A spy in your house.
A talkie that comes to stay.
A woman who always minds your business.
A woman who comes into the house voice first.
A woman who has a hot temper and a cold shoulder.
A woman who is never outspoken.
A woman who never goes without saying.
Another figure of speech, relatively speaking.
The speaker of the house.
What you inherit when you marry your wife, free of charge.

MOTION PICTURES:
A business that is never at a standstill.

MOTORIST:
A driver who. .
. . after seeing a wreck, drives carefully for a few blocks.
. . forgot that he used to be a pedestrian.
. . has either auto insurance or accidents.
. . not only takes good care of his car, he also keeps pedestrians in good running condition.
. . slows down as he passes a stop sign.

MOUNTAIN CLIMBER:
A man who. .
. . should always foot the bill.
. . should never lose himself in his work.
. . wants to take another peak.

MOUSE:
A creature that squeaks for itself.

MOUTH:
Another thing that often is opened by mistake.

MOVIE STAR:
A woman who. .
. . conceals her age but reveals her figure.
. . divorces her husband when she needs publicity.
. . goes to parties to show off her latest mink and her latest husband.
. . is usually in mink condition.

.. never knows where her next husband is coming from.

MOVIES:

A place where people talk behind your back.

A place where you spend $7 so that during intermission you can spend 75¢ for a 10¢ bar worth a nickel.

M.P.

Monthly payments.

MUD:

Something thicker than water.

MUFFLER:

A scarf worn over loud ties to silent them.

MULE:

An animal that can't pull while kicking, and can't kick while pulling

MUMMY:

An Egyptian who was pressed for time.

MUSHROOM:

A place where people neck.

MUSIC EXPERT:

One who, when he hears a lady singing in the bath, puts his ear to the keyhole.

MUSIC HATER:

A man who likes to hear songs without words sung to music without sound.

MUSICIAN:

A band aid.

A man who earns his living by playing around.

A man who helps many singers with his playing. He drowns them out.

A man who plays when he works and works when he plays.

MUSTARD:

The only thing that stays hot in the refrigerator.

MYSTERY:

A man whose last name is Ry.

MYTH:

A female moth.

A woman who hasn't got a husband.

N:

A letter in transit.

NAG:
A woman who remembers what her husband forgets.
An old horse, or woman depending whether it gallops
or gossips.

NAGGING WIFE:
The bitter half.

NAIL:
A small piece of iron that a man uses to aim at while
hitting his thumb.
The original coat hanger.

NAILS:
What a hardware dealer always has on hand.

NAIVE:
What you cut your meat with.

NAPKIN:
A lapcherchief.
A sleeping relative.

NAPOLEON:
A famous chocolate pastry.

NAUGHTY:
Having lots of zeros.

NECESSITY:
Something you can go without in order to make a down
payment on a luxury.

NECK:
Something which if you don't stick out, you won't get
into trouble up to.

NEGLIGEE:
What a woman hopes she'll have on when the house
burns down.

NEIGHBOR:
A person who. .
. . advises you what to buy so he can borrow it later.
. . buys things he can afford to show off to people who
can't appreciate them.
. . can watch you taking it easy without thinking you're
just lazy.
. . comes to your door and exchanges a little dirt for a
little sugar.
. . is always trying to borrow things.

. . is doing something you can't afford.

. . is here today and gone tomorrow.

. . knows more about your affairs than yourself.

. . will borrow your pot and then cook your goose.

. . will get to your house in two minutes and it will take him two hours to go back home.

. . wonders when your loud party will end.

NERO:

A Roman candleburner.

NERVE DOCTOR:

A tic Doc.

NERVE SPECIALIST:

A twitch doctor.

NET:

Holes ties together.

NET INCOME:

The money a fisherman makes.

NEUROTIC:

A man who, when you ask him how he feels in the morning, tells you.

A person who has discovered the secret of perpetual emotion.

A person who suffers from causes for which there is no disease.

NEW BABY:

Prince of Wales.

NEW YEAR'S EVE:

The only time of the year you blow your horn instead of your top.

NEW YEAR RESOLUTION:

Something that goes in one year and out the other.

NEW YORKER:

A man who gets acquainted with his neighbor by meeting him down in Florida.

A man who has never seen the Statue of Liberty or a parking space.

A man who will all but break his neck to save ten minutes he will waste anyhow.

NEWLYWED:

A man who puts up the storm windows the first time his wife suggests it.

NEWS:

The same old thing only it happened to different people.

NEWSPAPER:

Something that is black and white and read all over.

NEWSREEL:

A moving picture that shows real news.

NIAGARA FALLS:

Water on the rocks.

NIGHT:

A dark day.

NIGHT CLUB:

A place where. .

. . people go to eat, drink and be mentioned.

. . people go who are not hungry, to eat things they don't like, at prices they can't afford.

. . people with nothing to remember go to forget.

. . the cover charge covers nothing.

. . you pay a fancy figure for checking your hat.

NIGHT CLUB BOUNCER:

A man who throws noisy parties.

NIGHT WATCHMAN:

A man who hasn't worked a day in his life.

Yawn patrol.

NIGHTGOWN:

A dress a woman will never wear out.

NITRATE:

Usually lower than the day rate.

Rates for night time.

NITWIT:

A wise guy who knits.

NO MAN'S LAND:

The ladies lounge.

NOBODY:

A famous woman's husband.

NON-CONDUCTOR:

The motorman.

NONSTOP TALKER:

Earitation.

NOOSE:

What's in the papers.

NOSE:

A part of the human body that shines snubs, snoops and sneezes.

An organ that should be seen and not heard.

What a woman will talk through if you shut your mouth.

NOTHING:

A balloon with the skin peeled off.

Something many people are good for.

The best thing to do in a hurry.

The best thing to say when in doubt.

What a woman does when she wants smooth hands.

What most people know more about than anything else.

NOVELIST:

A man who writes something that truth is stranger than.

NOVELTY MANUFACTURER:

A person who lives off the fad of the land.

NUDISM:

Exposure with composure.

The only cult which gives you the bare facts.

NUDIST:

A person who. .

. . believes in altogetherness.

. . can tell you if it's raining without holding out his hand.

. . goes hatless, coatless and wears trousers to match.

. . has less pocket space than a sailor.

. . has nothing to hide.

. . has nothing to wear and goes around and wears it.

. . is wrapped up only in himself.

. . likes to go around in his silhouette.

. . on whom you can't pin anything.

. . peels first and gets sunburned afterwards.

. . suffers from clothestrophia.

. . worships the only suit which gives you the bare facts.

NUDIST CAMP:

A nude ranch.

A place where man and woman meet to air their differences.

A place where nothing goes on.

A place where people are all together in the altogether.

A place where the peeling is mutual.

A place where you get exposure with composure.

NUISANCE:

A man who is here today and here tomorrow.

A man you like better the more you see him less.

NULL:

Four-letter void.

NURSE:

A girl who holds your hand and expects your temperature to go down.

NURSERY:

A bawlroom.

Brat control.

Heir chamber.

NUTRITION:

What replaces oldrition.

OATH:

A promise not to tell somebody something.

OBESITY:

Surplus gone to waist.

OBOE:

An ill wind that nobody blows good.

OBSERVATORY:

A place where things are always looking up.

OCULIST:

A doctor you go to see when you can't see.

A man with an eye for business.

ODD:

Uneven.

OFFICE:

The place where you can relax from your strenuous home life.

OFFISH:

Where a tipsy secretary typsh.

OILY:

The opposite of late.

O.K

Yes in two words.

OLD AGE:

The period when your thoughts turn from passion to pension.

When it takes longer to rest than it does to get tired.

OLD CAR:

Junk wagon with fenders.

Tin can on wheels.

OLD MAID:

A girl who. .

. . can't find a YES man,

. . doesn't care WHO'S WHO or WHAT'S WHAT all she wants to know is WHEN WHEN.

. . failed to strike while the iron was hot.

. . has been good for nothing.

. . has been looked over and than overlooked.

. . is a lady in waiting.

. . is a lemon that never has been squeezed.

. . is a slipping beauty.

. . is 24 where she should be 36.

. . knows all the answers but nobody asked the question.

. . no's too much.

. . on hearing a whistle turns off the teakettle.

. . sure gave up before she gave in.

. . though she is a YES woman, never had a change to talk.

. . uses her phone only for outgoing calls.

. . waited so long for her ship to come in her pier collapsed.

OLD TIMER:

A man who remembers when. .

. . a baby was an addition and not a deduction.

. . a caller rang the doorbell instead of blowing his horn.

. . a car salesman said 500 he meant the price and not the horsepower.

. . a coffee break was your lunch hour.

. . a couple used to go driving in the park instead of parking in the drive.

. . a day's work took a day and not a week.

. . a dishwasher had to be married and not bought.

. . a dollar was worth fifty cents.

. . a hero meant a person and not a sandwich.

. . a man did his own witholding on his take-home pay.

. . a summer vacation was one day at the country fair.

. . a wife put food in cans instead of taking it out.

. . a wife's meals were carefully thought out rather than thawed out.

. . a woman married a man for his money instead of divorcing him for it.

. . air pollution was corned beef and cabbage.

. . an allergy was just an itch and all you did was scratch it.

. . baby sitters were called mothers.

. . bussing meant kissing instead of hauling kids around.

. . campers were people and not trucks.

. . dancing was done with the feet.

. . doctors used to smoke and kids didn't.

. . eight-forty was the time the movie started and not the price of the ticket.

. . five-and-ten stood for cents and not for dollars.

. . girls stayed home when they had nothing to wear.

. . health foods were whatever your mother said you'd better eat or else.

. . it cost more to run a car than park it.

. . it took a whole week to spend a week's pay.

. . people aimed to get to Heaven instead of to the moon.

. . people stopped spending when they ran out of money.

. . the wonder drugs of the day were Castor oil and camphor.

. . the younger generation used to go to bed before the adults.

. . we had trees on the street instead of parking meters.

. . we sat down at the table and counted our blessings instead of calories.

. . we used to kill time by working.

. . woman wore nightcaps instead of drinking them.

. . you were only broke the day before payday.

. . your coffee break came with the meal.

OLEOMAGARINE:

Food bought by people who have seen butter days.

ONE-WAY STREET:
A street in which a pedestrian is bumped from the rear only.

ONION:
Food that builds you up physically and drags you down socially.

Tear jerker.

OOZY:
Who is he?

OPERA:
A place where a guy gets stabbed in the back and instead of bleeding he sings.

A jukebox with chandelier.

An unerving series of catastrophes that usually ends up with a joyful chorus.

OPERA SINGER:
A person who is always telling his troubles.

OPERATION:
Something that takes hours to perform and years to describe.

OPERETTA:
A girl who works for the telephone company.

OPINION:
Something you have on your mind and want to get off your chest.

OPPORTUNIST:
A person who finds himself in hot water, takes a bath.

OPTICIAN:
A man who has an eye for business.

A man whose shop is a sight for sore eyes.

OPTIMIST:
A man who. .

. . asks his wife to help him with the supper dishes.

. . believes everything he reads on book jackets.

. . believe the thinning out of his hair is only a temporary matter.

. . buys a box of grass seed and a new lawn-mower the same day.

. . buys a lifetime pen and expects it to last at least a month.

. . counts his change while running for a bus.

. . doesn't give a darn what happens as long as it doesn't happen to him.

. . expects change from a taxi driver.

. . figures when his shoes wear out he'll be back on his feet.

. . gets married at 80 and then buys a house near a school.

. gets married on Independence Day.

. . goes with a fishing pole when he finds his basement floods.

. . goes into a hotel without luggage and asks to have a check cashed.

. . goes to a summer resort his friend has recommended.

. . is always able to laugh at your troubles.

. . is planning to spend the money left over after taxes.

. . keeps the motor running while his wife pops in to buy a new hat.

. . keeps the motor running while waiting for his wife to get dressed.

. . lights a match before asking for a cigarette.

. . looks for pork in a can of pork and beans.

. . looks forward to enjoying the scenery on a detour.

. . makes 500 a week and marries a girl who is crazy about children.

. . marries his secretary and thinks he will continue dictating to her.

. . opens a hat shop before the mirrors are delivered.

. . plays gin rummy with his wife.

. . says he's only going to watch the start of the late, late TV show.

. . sends a package by parcel post and marks it RUSH.

. . sets aside two hours to do his income tax return.

. . sits in the tenth row and winks at the chorus girl.

. . spends his last dollar to buy a new wallet.

. . takes a camera along when he goes fishing.

. . takes a frying pan along on his fishing trip.

. . tells you to cheer up when things are going his way.

. . thinks a woman will hang up the phone just because she said goodbye.

.. thinks he can build a $200,000 house for $200,000.

.. thinks he has no bad habits.

.. thinks he will never do anything stupid again.

.. thinks marriage will end his troubles.

.. thins that a word to his wife is sufficient.

.. thinks the woman he is going to marry is better than the one he just divorced.

.. went to court to find out when his marriage license expires.

.. will leave his door unlocked hoping his wife will walk out on him.

.. wipes off his glasses before starting to eat a grapefruit.

OPTIMIST:

A woman who. .

.. calls a bulge a curve.

.. powders her nose before she looks under the bed.

OPTOMETRIST:

A site for sore eyes.

OPTOMETRIST IN ALASKA:

An optical Aleutian.

ORANGE:

A fruit that doesn't rhyme with anything.

ORANGE JUICE:

Liquid vitamins.

ORATOR:

A fellow who's always ready to lay down your life for his country.

A man with a few thousand words.

ORCHESTRA CONDUCTOR:

A man who isn't afraid to face the music.

ORGANIC:

Kind of music played in church.

ORIENTAL GROCERY CLERK:

A Chinese checker.

OSTEOPATH:

A man who puts a lot of feeling into his work.

A man who rubs you the right way.

OTTER:

Opposite of inner.

OTTOMAN:

A car mechanic.

OUTDOOR MAN:
A man who hammers on the radiator for more steam while dressing to go skiing.

OUTPATIENT:
A person who has fainted.

OVEREATING:
An activity which will make you thick to your stomach.

OVERTIME:
Salary with a fringe on top.

OX:
A cow that can't have babies.
What you chop your wood with.

OYSTER:
A fish that built like a nut.

P.
A letter that's always in place.

PAINLESS DENTIST:
One who forgets to send the bill.

PAINTING:
Expensive wallpaper.
Some which, when well done, is rare.

PAJAMAS:
An article of clothing you take along on a honeymoon in case of fire.

PAL:
A fellow who lends you money.

PANHANDLER:
A beggar that loafs or a loafer that begs.

PANTOMINE:
A time when people talk but say nothing as usual.

PAPER HANGAR:
A person whose business is a put-up job.

PAPERWEIGHT:
Something to keep all your bills down.

PARACHUTE:
Something that doesn't mean a thing if you don't pull the string.

PARADOX:
A man walking a mile and only moving two feet.

Any two doctors seen together.

PARISH:

How drunks pronounce the French capital.

PAROLE:

A cell-out.

PARKING LOT:

A place where you leave your car to have dents put in the fenders.

PARKING METER:

A place where a car stops on a dime.

PARKING SPACE:

A space where another car is parked.

A space that disappears while you make a U-turn.

An unoccupied space along the curb on the other side of the street.

PARROTS HOSPITAL:

A polly clinic.

PARSLEY:

The food you push aside to see what's under it.

PASSENGER:

A person who is told where to get off.

PASSION:

Love in bloom.

PASSPORT PHOTO:

A way to see yourself as others see you.

PASTEURIZE:

Too far to see.

PATIENCE:

Postponed temper.

PATRIOT:

A fellow who is always ready to lay down your life for his country.

PAUPER:

The man who married Mama.

PAWNBROKER:

A man for whom it's never too late to lend.

A man you have to put up with.

A man you have to see after you've done business with your stockbroker.

A man who hopes you will see him at your earliest inconvenience.

A man who takes great interest in serving the poor.

A time keeper.

PAWNSHOP:

Instant money.

PEA:

A vegetable pill.

PEACE:

Something that rages through the post-war world.

Something we all are fighting for.

PEACEMAKER:

Spat remover.

PEACH:

An apple that needs a shave.

A smooth fruit with a heart of stone.

PEACOCK:

Turkey in full bloom.

Technicolor turkey.

PEDESTRIAN:

A case of survival of the fittest.

A girl who doesn't neck.

A motorist with three good tires.

A person who always has that run down feeling.

A person who always has the right of wait.

A person who counted on his wife to put some gas in the car.

A person who doesn't know where his next car is coming from.

A person who falls by the wayside.

A person who has failed to keep up his car payments.

A person who finally found a parking space.

A person who just bought a used car.

A person who has learned it doesn't pay to go straight.

A person who has the right of way when he is in an ambulance.

A person who has two cars and a wife and a son.

A person who ignored his wife when she asked for a second car.

A person who is always found in front of cars.

A person who is here today and run-down tomorrow.
A person who is looking for the place he parked the car.
A person who is safe only when he is riding.
A person who should be seen and not hurt.
A person who thought his battery would last another day.
A person whose son is home from college.
A person whose wife beat him to the garage.
A street walking object invisible to the motorist.
One who leaps before he looks.
The vanishing American.

PEEPING TOM:
A night watchman.
A peak freak.
A window fan.
A wolf, window shopping.

PELICAN:
A bird that always fills the bill.

PEN NAME:
A prisoner's serial number.

PENTHOUSE:
A place where you have a roof under your feet.

PERFECT SUMMER DAY:
A day when the sun is shining, the breeze is blowing, the birds are singing and the lawn mower is broken.

PERFECT APPLIANCE:
Something too heavy for the neighbors to borrow.

PEFECTIONIST:
Someone who takes great pains and gives them to other people.

PERFUME:
A pretty gift that cost man a pretty penny.
A sweet odor that holds you smellbound.
A wife tenderizer.

PERFUME SHOP:
The scenter of town.

PERFUME SMUGGLER:
A fragrant violator.

PERIOD:
A comma that has curled up and gone to sleep.

PERPETUAL MOTION:
A cow drinking a pail of milk.
The family upstairs.

PESSIMIST:
A man who. .
.. always does better today than he expects to do to-morrow.
.. always finds something to worry about once he puts his mind to it.
.. believes that life is neither worth living nor leaving.
.. blows out the candles to see how dark it is.
.. buys more than one life-time pen.
.. complains about the noise when opportunity knocks.
.. constantly keeps his bad breaks relined.
.. crosses his fingers when he says; Good Morning!
.. crosses the street and his fingers at the same time.
.. crosses the street twice to be a double-crosser.
.. expects nothing on a silver platter except tarnish.
.. expects to find bad news in a fortune cookie.
.. feels bad when he feels good for fear that he'll feel worse when he feels better.
.. forgets to laugh, while an optimist laughs to forget.
.. is a disappointed optimist.
.. is a misfortune teller.
.. is a reformed optimist.
.. is afraid the optimist is right.
.. is happy when he is wrong.
.. is never happy unless he is miserable.
.. is seasick during the entire voyage of life.
.. lives with an optimist.
.. looks both ways before crossing a one-way street.
.. sees a cloud in every silver lining.
.. sees only the hole in the doughnut.
.. thinks if he reaches down to pick up a four-leaf clover he will probably be bitten by a snake.
.. thinks no trouble is as bad as no trouble.
.. wears a belt as well as suspenders.
.. when he has the choice of two evils, chooses both.
.. would ask in a Chinese restaurant for a misfortune cookie.

PEST:

A person who wants to talk to you when you want to read and reads when you want to talk.

PETITION:

A list of people who didn't have the nerve to say NO.

PETTING:

A study of anatomy in braille.

A ticklish proposition.

PHARMACIST:

A man in a white coat who stands behind a sofa fountain selling $5 watches.

PHARMACY:

A department store with a prescription counter.

PHEASANT:

A turkey in technicolor.

PHEASANT UNDER GLASS:

A very small bird with a very large bill.

PHILOSOPHER:

A man who always knows what to do until it happens to him.

A man who can look at an empty glass with a smile.

A man who doesn't care if both parties to an argument are wrong.

A man who knows that nothing ages a woman as fast as trying to stay young.

PHILOSOPHICAL:

The cheerful attitude assumed by everybody not directly involved in the trouble.

PHILANTHROPIST:

A man who gives away what he should give back.

PHILATELIST:

An eccentric person who pays more for used stamps than for new ones.

PHONY:

A guy who tries to slash his wrist with an electric razor.

PHOTOGRAPH:

A sitting image of you.

What you have to take before you can get.

PHOTOGRAPHER:

A man who can make an ugly girl pretty as a picture.

PHYSICAL EDUCATION:
What a young man gets when he goes to the beach.
PHYSICIAN:
A fancy schmantzy name for a doctor.
PICNIC:
A snack in the grass.
An affair where you smack your lips over food at which
     you'd turn up your nose at home.
An ant lunch.
PICKET:
A man who walks for a living.
PICKLE:
A cucumber in a sour mood.
PICKPOCKET:
A man who. .
. . believes that every crowd has a silver lining.
. . is a garment worker.
. . is a trouser browser.
. . is a wallet collector.
. . is all the time finding things before people lose them.
. . never knows where his next steal is coming from.
. . will always extend a helping hand.
. . will always pick his way through a crowd.
PIECE DE RESISTANCE:
French for tough streak.
PIGGY BANK:
A place where the head of the house gets bus money a
     day before payday.
PILLOW:
A napsack.
Headquarter.
PILOT'S LICENSE:
Fly paper.
PIN MONEY:
Bowling fee.
PINEAPPLE:
A fruit so called because it's neither a pine nor an apple.
PIRACY:
Shiplifting.
PIZZA:

Fried manhole cover.
PLACE MAT:
Lunching pad.
PLANNED PARENTHOOD:
Kid mapping.
PLASTIC SURGEON:
A doctor who aims to please.
PLATONIC FRIENDSHIP:
The interval between the introduction and the first kiss.
PLAYBOY:
A man who. .
. . always sees nightspots before his eyes.
. . doesn't know what he wants and gets plenty of it.
. . finds it easy to make both weekends meet.
. . lives date-to-date existance.
PLAYPEN:
Rattle trap.
PLEASURE TRIP:
Going away without your wife.
Taking the kids to camp.
Taking your mother-in-law to the station.
PLUMBER:
A drain surgeon.
A man who gets paid for sleeping under other peo-
    ple's sinks.
A man who makes a living when the spirit is willing but
    the flush is weak.
PLUMBER APPRENTICESHIP:
Basic draining.
PLURAL:
The same as singular only more of it.
POCKET:
A bag in your clothes.
A little place where you put little things.
PODIATRIST:
A doctor who bills the foot.
A doctor who is always down at the heels.
A doctor who knows his bunions.
A doctor who makes money hand over feet.
POETRY:

160

Reading matter where every line begins with a capital
letter.

POINTER:

A sic dog.

POISE:

The ability to keep talking while the other fellow picks
up the check.

The art of raising the eyebrows instead of the roof.

POISON IVY:

Something that starts from scratch and itches all over.

The only thing that you meet that you never know
you've met until two days after you met it.

POKER LOSS:

Chip wreck.

POLICEMAN:

A never present help in time of trouble.

POLICEMAN'S UNIFORM:

A lawsuit.

POLITICIAN:

A man who. .

. . Always saddles a question.

. . borrows your pot to cook your goose.

. . can give you complete attention without hearing a
word you say.

. . can sit on a fence and keep both ears to the ground.

. . can talk for an hour without mentioning what he was
talking about.

. . changes sides more often than a windshield wiper.

. . divides his time between running for office and running
for cover.

. . doesn't mean what he says and doesn't say what he
means.

. . faces every question with an open mouth.

. . finds out which way the crowd is going, then jumps in
front and carries the flag.

. . gets into the public eye by getting in the public's hair.

. . has his hands in your pocket, his mouth in your ear,
and his faith in your patience.

. . if he can't say anything bad about his opponent, won't
say anything at all.

161

. . is always for the people but against the public.

. . is knows as a dealer in promises.

. . is so busy he has no time to be honest.

. . knows how to say nothing, just doesn't always know when.

. . needs three hats; one he tosses in the ring, one to talk through and one he eats.

. . plays both sides against the taxpayer.

. . says, "Nice to see you again," even if he has never seen you before.

. . shakes your hand before election and pulls your leg afterwards.

. . takes money from the rich and votes from the poor, and promises both sides protection from each other.

. . tells you who to vote for.

. . will stand for anything that will leave him sitting pretty.

An orator improperly wired.

POLLS:

Voting places where you stand in line for a chance to decide who will spend your money.

POLLUTION:

An air cache.

Grime on the street.

POLO:

Horseplay.

Hockey on horseback.

Snobby hobby.

POLYGON:

An absent parrot.

PONY:

A junior horse.

POODLE:

What you step into when it rains cats and dogs.

POPCORN:

Dad's old jokes.

POPULAR PERFUME:

Best smeller.

POPULAR WINTER SPORT:

Taking a plane to Florida.

POPULATION EXPLOSION:
Birthquake.
Love in bloom.
PORCUPINE:
A pin cushion with legs.
PORK:
Meat used in chicken salad.
PORTFOLIO:
A long brief case.
POST OFFICE:
A place that launches a thousand zips.
Stamping ground.
POSTMAN:
A man from whom all girls get love letters.
POST-OPERATIVE:
A letter carrier.
POSTSCRIPT:
The only thing readable in a woman's letter.
POVERTY:
The only thing money can't buy.
PRACTICAL JOKER:
One who aims to tease.
PRACTICAL NURSE:
A nurse who marries her rich patient.
PRAISE:
What people are most dangerous with because it costs nothing.
What the vicar does.
What you get after you are dead.
PREACHER:
The only man who can keep dozens of women quiet for an hour.
PREMATURE:
A baby born before its parents are married.
PRESIDENT:
A cabinet maker.
PRETZEL MAKER:
One who earns a living in a crooked dough.
PRIEST:

The only man who remains a bachelor no matter how many women he marries.

PRISM:

A place for light waves that commit minor refractions.

PRISONER:

The only person who doesn't mind being interrupted in the middle of a sentence.

PRIVATE TUTOR:

Hire education.

PROCRASTINATION:

Putting off one's problem for a brainy day.

PRODUCER:

A man who gives the public what they want and hopes they want it

PROFESSIONAL:

A man who makes a living out of what others do for pleasure.

PROFESSOR:

A man who goes to college and never gets out.

A man who talks in other people's sleep.

PROMISE:

The only thing a person can keep by giving it to someone else.

PROOF READER:

A galley slave.

A type righter.

PROPAGANDA:

Baloney disguised as food for thought.

PROSPERITY:

A period when people go into debt for things they don't need.

A period when people make more money than they earn and spend more than they make.

A period when we all have twice as much money and it buys half as much.

PROSE:

Paid athletes.

PROVERB:

A short sentence based on long experience.

PRUNE:

A plum that has seen better days.
PSYCHIATRIST:
A man who. .
. . doesn't have to worry as long as others do.
. . goes to a burlesque show to watch the audience.
. . goes to a movie and understands the picture.
. . if he didn't have a medical degree, would be considered just plain nosey.
. . makes money using other people's heads.
. . makes you crazy, then makes you pay $500 to prove it.
. . tells people how to stand on their own feet while reclining on couches.
. . when a pretty girl enters a crowded room, looks at everybody else.
. . will listen to you as long as you don't make sense.
A couch coach.
A doctor who can't stand the sight of blood.
A doctor with a couch.
A head coach.
A mental detective.
A mental peeping Tom.
A mental pickpocket.
A mind sweeper.
A nut cracker.
The last person you talk to before you start talking to yourself.
PSYCHIATRY:
A sick oak.
The only business where the customer is always wrong.
PSYCHOLOGIST:
A man who tells you what you have known already-in-words that you don't understand.
PSYCHOLOGY:
A word of four syllables that you throw into the conversation to distract attention when you got yourself cornered and can't explain your way out.
PSYCHOPATH:
A sick road.
PUBERTY:

165

The period when children stop asking questions and begin to question answers.

PUBLIC OPINION:
What people think other people think.

PUBLIC SPEAKING:
The art of diluting a two-minute idea with a two-hour vocabulary.

PUBLICIST:
Paid piper.

PUNCH LINE:
A group of people waiting in line for a drink from the bowl.

PUNCTURE:
A little hole found in tires a long distance from garages.

PUP TENT:
A portable doghouse.

PUPPY:
A junior dog.

PUSH:
Something that will get you everywhere—except through a door marked PULL.

PYRAMID:
An organized pile of rocks.

Q:
What quarrel always begins with.

QUADRUPLETS:
Four crying out loud.

QUARTET:
A group of four, each of whom thinks the other three can't sing.

QUEEN BEE:
The power behind the drone.

QUIET:
Silent noise.

RABBIT FARMER:
Hare raiser.

RACE:
To run for a price.

RACEHORSE:

An animal that can take several thousand people for a ride at the same time.

RACETRACK:
A place where windows clean people.

RADIATOR:
A heating device which remains cold when banged on.

RADICAL:
A conservative out of a job.

RADIO:
A chatter box.

A device that sounds fine in your home and terrible next door.

A jukebox with commercials.

Television without a picture screen.

RADIO ANNOUNCER:
A man who talks until you have a headache, then tries to sell you something to relieve it.

RADIO COMEDIAN:
A network nitwit.

RADIO SERIAL:
Something you can tune in once a year without losing any of the story.

RAILROAD DINER:
A chew-chew car.

RAIN:
Something that, when you take an umbrella it doesn't.

RAIN GAUGE:
Dew tell.

RAISIN:
A grape that worried too much and got wrinkled.

RANCH:
A chicken farm with horses.

RARE:
The steak you ordered well-done.

RARE SIGHT:
A man trying to get to first base with an old bat.

RARE VOLUME:
A borrowed book that comes back.

RATS:
Cheese eating bloodhounds.

RAVING BEAUTY:
A girl who came out last in a beauty contest.

REAL ESTATE OFFICE:
Deed letter office.

REALTOR:
A man who has a lot on his mind.

RECESS:
Teacher's coffee break.

RECESSION:
A depression that got side-tracked by prosperity.

A lull between two booms.

Income poop.

RECIPE:
A note you follow in cooking.

A pattern for cooking.

RECREATION:
Any work you don't have to do for a living.

RED:
What an impatient driver sees when he stops for a traffic light.

REDCAP:
The only man who makes money at the track.

REDUCING EXERCISE:
Shaking the head from side to side when offered a second helping.

REDUCING EXPERT:
One who lives on the fat of the land.

REDUCING MACHINE:
Something that cost so much, you have to starve yourself to keep up the payments.

REDUCING SALON:
Slim gym.

Thinner sanctum.

REFINEMENT:
Yawning with your mouth closed.

REFRIGERATOR:
A place where you store leftovers until they're old enough to be thrown away.

REGATTA:
Sails meeting.

REHEARSAL:
Acting under orders.

REINDEER:
A horse with a hatrack.
An animal with a TV antenna.

RELATIVE:
An inherited critic.
People who come to dinner who aren't friends.

RELIEF:
Taking off your tight shoes.

RENDEZVOUS:
A dated date.

RENO:
A place where people go to kick the marriage habit.
A place where the cream of the crop goes through the separator.
A separation center.
The great divide.
The land of the free and the grave of the home.
The last mile of the wedding march.
The residence of the bitter half.
The Sue City.

REPORT CARD:
A poison letter written by a school teacher.

REPORTS:
Time-consuming paperwork.

RESEARCH:
Getting facts out of old books people never read and putting them into new books nobody will read.
What people do when they can't find what they are looking for.
When you look for something twice.

RESORT:
A place where nobody knows how unimportant you are at home.
A place where the tired grow more tired.

RESTAURANT:
A filling station.
A place where people grab, gab, gobble and gulp.

RETIRED TENANT:

Idle roomer.
RETIREMENT:
Twice as much husband on half as much pay.
RETREAT:
An army term meaning to advance in the direction you
just came from.
REUNION:
A group of people getting together to see who's fall-
ing apart.
REVIEW:
What a military parades passes in.
RHODE ISLAND:
Texas after taxes.
RHUBURB:
Bloodshot celery.
Celery with high blood pressure.
Celery with a sunburn.
RHUMBA:
A dance done mostly south of the border.
Hip language.
RICH RELATIVE:
The kin we love to touch.
The type of people who live the longest.
RIGHT:
A word that's usually spelled right.
RING:
A hole with a border around it.
ROAD MAP:
A book of etiquette showing motorists which fork to
use.
A device for finding out what road you should have
taken.
A map that tells you everything except how to fold it
again.
A piece of paper that helps you get lost.
ROCK 'N ROLL MUSIC:
Earitation.
ROLLER-SKATE SALE:
Cheap skates.
ROMANCE:

An affair that begins by splashing at waterfalls and ends over a leaky faucet.

Ants in Rome.

Anything that ends in a wedding.

Something like a game of chess. One wrong move and you're mated.

ROOF:

Something every house should have in case of rain.

ROOMING HOUSE:

A place where roomers spread rumors about other roomers.

ROOSTER:

A feathered alarm clock.

ROTISSERIE:

A ferris wheel for chicken.

ROULETTE:

A wheel that seldom takes a turn for the better.

ROYAL BLOOD:

Blue genes.

RUBBERS:

Something that if your feet are dry you haven't walked in the rain without.

RUG:

Something that's being sold by the yard and worn by the feet.

RUMMAGE SALE:

A place where you buy stuff from somebody else's attic to store in your own.

RUMOR:

Something nobody believes until it's officially denied.

Something that goes in one ear and out the other.

Something that isn't safe to repeat but often juicy to hear.

RUSH HOUR:

Solidified traffic.

The hour when traffic is at a stand still.

RUSSIAN:

One who sits on nothing and dances.

SABLE:

The skin girls love to touch.

171

SADDLE:
The only sure thing on a horse.

SAFETY ZONE:
A place where a car can hit you only from one side.

SAILOR:
A man who makes his living on water but never touches it on shore.

SALARY:
An income which is always short of the cost of living.
An unearned income.

SALE:
Where a woman ruins one dress to buy another.

SALES RESISTANCE:
The triumph of mind over matter.

SALES TALK:
Trade wind.

SALESMAN:
A man with a smile, a shine on his shoes and a lousy territory.

SALMON:
A herring with red underwear.

SALT:
Something that makes potatoes taste bad if you haven't got any.

SANCTITY:
What they did at the Boston Tea Party.

SANDWICH SPREAD:
What you get when you eat between meals.

SARCASM:
Getting an edge in wordwise.
Quip lash.

SARONG:
A brightly colored potato sack-for tomatoes.
A dishtowel that finally found an interesting place to work.
Itsa not right.

SAUSAGE:
A hamburger in tights.
Hash in cellophane pants.

SAVING:

Doing without what you need in order to have money for something you can do without.

SCAMPOO:
A quick rinse.

SCANDALMONGER:
A person who put who and who together and gets whew!

SCARED FLOWER ARRANGER:
A petrified florist.

SCARED SKIN-DIVER:
Chicken of the sea.

SCHOOL:
A place where kids go to catch colds from other kids so they can stay home.

The stuff between holidays.

SCIENTIST:
A man who calls ordinary things by such longer names that you think he's talking about something else.

A man who can rave about nylons when they are empty.

A man who is always trying to prolong life so we can have time to pay for all the gadgets he invents.

A man who works himself to death so that he will be remembered after his death.

SCOTCH:
A beverage that makes the world go round.

A beverage that makes you see double and feel single.

A beverage that tastes so bad, that, if it wasn't so expensive, nobody would drink it.

SCOTLAND CHEESE:
Loch Ness Muenster.

SCREEN DOOR:
Something kids get a bang out of.

SCULPTOR:
A poor unfortunate who makes faces and busts.

SEA HORSE:
Filly of flounder.

SEASHORE:
A place where young girls are looking for husbands , and husbands are looking for young girls.

SEASICKNESS:

A trouble that makes you forget all other troubles.
Ocean motion notion.
SECONDHAND BOOKS:
Twice-sold tales.
SECOND MARRIAGE:
The triumph of curiosity over experience.
SECOND STORY MAN:
The fellow whose wife doesn't believe his first story.
SECRETION:
The tendency to hide things!
SECRETS:
Anything a woman doesn't know.
Something a woman tells everybody not to tell anybody.
Something it takes a lot of women to keep.
Something that's hushed about from place to place.
Something you tell one woman at a time.
The only thing some women give away.
Things we give to other people to keep for us.
What a woman can keep with telling effect.
SECRET AGENT:
A man who holds his job as long as he holds his tongue.
SECRETARY:
A girl to whom you pay a salary while she's killing time between night school and marriage.
A stenographer who runs the boss.
A woman who must look like a girl, think like a man, act like a lady and work like a horse.
A woman who seldom can act but can always distract.
SELF-MADE MAN:
Usually a pathetic example of unskilled labor.
SERMON:
A moralogue.
A religious pep-talk.
Soul food.
SERVICE STATION:
A place where you fill your car and drain the family.
SEWING CENTER:
Stitching post.
SEWING CIRCLE:

A place where women go to needle each other.

7-COURSE MEAL:
A martini with six olives.

SEX:
The most fun you can have without laughter.
The number after five.

SHADOW:
The only thing that never casts a shadow.

SHEPHERD:
A goat getter.

SHISH KABOB:
A goulash lollipop.
Mean popsicle.
Stew on a stick.

SHOE SHINER:
A bootician.

SHOE MAKER:
The only man who can call his sole his own.

SHOPLIFTING:
Free enterprise.

SHOPPER:
A person who goes buy-buy.

SHOPPING:
To buy or not to buy.

SHORT CUT:
A route on which you can't find anybody to ask where you are.

SHORT VACACTION:
A half a loaf.

SHOTGUN WEDDING:
A case of wife or death.

SHOULDER STRAP:
A piece of ribbon which keeps an attraction from becoming a sensation.

SHOWER:
A vertical bath.

SICK CROCODILE:
An illigator.

SIESTA:
Droop therapy.

SIGHTSEEING TRIP:
Guided hustle.
SIGN PAINTER:
A man of letters.
SILENCE:
The noise you don't hear when you listen.
SILK TIES:
The only thing that attracts spaghetti sauce.
SILLY GAME:
One your wife can beat you at.
SIMMER:
The season after spring.
SINKING FUND:
The average bank account.
SKELETON:
A man with his inside out and his outside off.
A stack of bones with all the people scraped off.
A stripteaser who overdid it.
SKI INSTRUCTOR:
A person whose business is always on the down-grade.
SKY-WRITING:
An air-brained scheme.
SKIER:
Two pieces of small wood with a person on top.
SKIING:
A sport that is best when you have lots of snow and plenty of Blue Cross.
A sport that people learn in several sittings.
A sport where you start on the top and work your way down.
SKIN:
The only thing you can occupy without paying rent.
SKIN SPECIALIST:
Itch doctor.
SKIP:
What a prisoner will do if you give him enough rope.
SKUNK:
A pussy cat with fluid drive.
Nasal appraisal.
SLANG:

Talk stranger than diction.

SLEEP:

An excellent way of listening to an opera.

Something that always seems more important the morning after that it did the night before.

The best cure for insomnia.

The best cure for worrying provided you do it instead.

What you don't know you are doing when you are and wish you could when you can't.

When you don't get enough the night before, you wake half a.

SLEEPING BAG:

A giant napsack.

SLEEPING CAR CONDUCTOR:

Berth control supervisor.

SLEEPWALKER:

The only person who gets his rest and exercise at the same time.

SMALL ANCHOR:

A little sinker.

SMALL BOY:

A restless noise with dirt on it.

SMART COOKIE:

A girl who starts out with a little slip and ends up with a while new wardrobe.

A wise cracker.

SMART DOCTOR:

A doctor who gives you a year to live and ten months to pay your bill.

SMARK DUCK:

A wise quacker.

SMOKERS:

People who, the more they fume, the less they fret.

SMORGASBORD:

Eatcetera.

SMOTHER:

It's Ma!

SNACK:

The pause that refreshes.

SNEEZING:

Much ado about nothing.

SNOB:
A person who walks like he's balancing the family tree on his nose.

SNORER:
A sound sleeper.

SNORING:
Just sleeping out loud.
Sheet music.

SNOW:
God's dandruff.
Rain a la mode.

SNUFF:
Stuff that, if you don't feel well, you're not quite up to.

SOAP OPERA:
Corn on the sob.

SOBER:
What you are when you can lie down on the floor without holding on.

SOCIAL CLIMBER:
Class hopper.

SOCIAL SECURITY:
A system that guarantees you a steak after your teeth are gone.

SOCIAL SECURITY CHECK:
Month to month resuscitation.

SOCIAL TACT:
Making your company feel at home, even though you wish they were.

SOCIETY PLAYBOY:
Cashanova.

SOCIOLOGIST:
A fellow who tells you stuff you already know in words you can't understand.

SOCKS:
Short stockings usually worn too long.
What a man throws away when they are not worth a darn.

SODA JERK:
A licensed fizzician.

SOFA:
A convertible without wheels.
A long way.

SOUP:
Stuff if you blow on, it becomes cooler faster than if you don't.

SOURPUSS:
A cat that has fallen into the vinegar.

SOUTHPAW:
A man who raises his children in the South.

SOUVENIRS:
Far-fetched junk.

SOVIET:
What the Russians say when they've finished dinner.

SPA:
A waterhole with vitamins.

SPACE:
The only thing some people take up in school.
The stuff thermos bottles are filled with.

SPAGHETTI:
A long thin slippery macaroni.
Stringy food that you wind around your fork and drop on your lap.

SPALEENGE:
A bad spelling of spelling.

SPANKING:
Stern punishment.

SPARROW:
A brunette canary.

SPAT:
Petty clash.

SPECIALIST:
A doctor who has patients trained to become ill only during office hours.
A man who concentrates more and more on less and less.

SPELL:
Something that if a stenographer can, she'll never be out of work for a long.

SPICE:

179

The plural of spouse.

SPILT MILK:
Udder waste.

SPINSTER:
A lady in waiting.

SPONGE:
An absorbing subject.
The only thing that's full of holes yet holds water.

SPOUSE:
A former lover.

SPRING:
The season of balls—golf, tennis, base and moth.

SPRING CLEANING:
The time when you rearrange the dust.

SPY:
National peeper.

SQUARE:
A circle with four corners.

SQUATTER:
One who takes a lot for granted.

SQUEAKING SCARF:
A noisy muffler.

STABLE:
A horse hotel.

STAGE FRIGHT:
Podium panic.

STAGNATION:
A country without women.

STAIN:
What I do when it rains

STALEMATE:
A dull spouse.
A husband who keeps telling the same jokes.
Ex-husband.
Last season's girlfriend.

STAMP ALBUM:
The only place where all nations can stick together.

STAR SPANGLED MANNER:
The only piece of music the public will stand for.
The song nobody knows.

STATESMAN:
A politician away from home.
STATIC:
Numbers looking for an argument.
STATION WAGON:
A vehicle a city person buys when he moves to the country so the country people will know he's from the city.
STATUE:
A pigeon depository.
Does that happen to be you?
STEAM:
Water gone crazy with the heat.
STENOGRAPHER:
A girl you teach how to spell while she's looking for a husband.
STEWARD:
A floating waiter.
STEWARDESS:
A flying waitress.
A tipless waitress.
Plane girl.
A girl who has to smile coast to coast.
STITCH:
A few in time saves embarrassing exposure.
STOCK BROKER:
Risk jockey.
A man who runs your fortune into a shoestring.
STOCK MARKET:
A place where people make and lose money nobody ever had.
STOCKHOLDER:
A man who is known by the company he keeps.
STOCKINGS:
Something that runs while a woman walks.
STOCKS:
A commodity bought and sold. If you win, it's an investment, if you lose, a speculation.
STOMACH:
A place you put your food when you eat.

STORE DETECTIVE:
Counter spy.
STORY TELLER:
A person who has a good memory and hopes other people don't.
STRAIGHT:
Without ginger ale.
STRAIGHT LINE:
The shortest distance between two points.
STRAPLESS BATHING SUIT:
A compromise between the law of gravity and the law of decency.
STRAPLESS GOWN:
A dress with no visible means of support.
STRATEGY:
It's when you keep firing after you're out of ammunition.
STREET:
A city road torn up by fast drivers and slow contractors.
STREET CLEANER:
A man who has to keep his mind in the gutter.
A rubble rouser.
STRENGTH OF MIND:
A person who can eat one salted peanut.
STRIP TEASER:
A girl who has everything and shows it.
A girl who is unsuited in her work.
A girl who looks good in everything she takes off.
STUCCO:
What you get when you sit on a gummo.
STUFFED OLIVE:
A grape with a tail light.
STUPID ANT:
Igno-rant.
STUPID RULER:
A ding-a-ling king.
SUBMARINE:
A boat that sinks on purpose.
A boat with water on all four sides.
And ordinary boat that dunks.

182

SUBURB:

A place where families go to live beyond the smog, the traffic, the crowd and their income.

A place where houses are farther apart and the payments closer together.

A place where the housewife wears shorts except when she puts on a dress to go into the city to buy a dress to go to the city in.

A place where the station wagons are bigger than the station.

SUBWAY:

A place so crowded that even the men can't all get seats.

A place where you put money in a machine and get taken for a ride.

SUCCESS:

When you have a credit card for every restaurant but your doctor won't let you eat.

When you have your name in everything but the telephone book.

Good fortune that comes from aspiration, perspiration and inspiration.

SUCCESSFUL SALEMAN:

A man who sells products that don't come back, to customers who do.

SUGAR:

White sand.

SUICIDE:

The last thing a man would do.

SUIT OF ARMOR:

A knightgown.

A man can.

SUITCASE:

Something to sit on while waiting for the train.

SUMMER:

The time when. .

. . children slam doors they left open all winter.

. . it is too hot to do the jobs it was too cold to do all winter.

. . my neighbor returns the bottle of cough medicine and borrows my suntan lotion.

. . kids are out of school, and mothers are out of their minds.

. . people come back from their vacation to rest up on their jobs.

. . the days get longer and the underwear shorter.

. . there is not much on radio, TV, or the girls on the beach.

. . they close all roads and open the detours.

. . you don't want to do all those things you've been wanting to do all winter.

. . you ride bumper to bumper to get to the beach where you sit the same way.

. . you try to keep your house as cold as it was in the winter when you complained about it.

SUMMER CAMP:

A place where kids get poison ivy the first day and spend the rest of the summer scratching.

A place where little boys go for mother's vacation.

SUMMER RESORT:

A place where. .

. . guests are welcome with open palms.

. . guest often give up good dollars for poor quarters.

. . nobody knows how unimportant you are at home.

. . people flock in great numbers to avoid each other.

. . the mosquitoes bite and the fish don't.

. . the tired grow more tired.

. . they charge you enough to make up for the ten months you're not there.

. . they get you coming and going.

SUN:

Skylight.

SUN BATHING:

A fry in the ointment.

SUN BURN:

A rib roast.

SUN GLASSES:

Optical seclusion.

SUNDAY PUNCH:

Drinks left over from Saturday night.

SUPERMARKET:

Shopping a la cart.

The only place where a housewife puts all her eggs in one basket.

A place where you spend 30 minutes hunting for instant coffee.

SUPERVISOR:

A man who can step on your toes without messing up your shine.

SURFER:

Man overboard.

SURGEON:

A doctor who knows people inside out.

A doctor who is a big fish.

Rushing forward.

SURLY:

It's not late.

SURPLUS:

A shortage of shortages.

Something you have no need for.

SWEATER:

A garment worn by a child when his mother feels chilly.

SWIMMER:

A pool shark.

SWIMMING INSTRUCTOR:

A hold-up man.

SWIMMING POOL:

A crowd of people with water in between.

SYMETRY:

Notice my oak!

SYMPATHY:

An artificial sym.

SYNONYM:

A word used when you can't spell the other.

A word that means the same but different.

TACT:

Getting your point across without stabbing someone with it.

Something you thought but didn't say.

The ability to make your guests feel at home, when you
   wish they were.
The ability to shut your mouth before someone wants
   to.
The fine part of knowing how far is too far.
The knack of making a point without making an enemy.
Keeping tongue in cheek.

TAIL:
Happy ending.

TAILOR:
A man who is always willing to suit you.

TANTRUM:
Gripes of wrath.

TAVERN:
Bottle ground.
Thirst-aid station.

TAX COLLECTOR:
A man looking for untold wealth.
A man who has what it takes to take what you have.

TAX EXPERT:
A man who keeps out of jail by putting you in the poorhouse.

TAX FORM:
Exploding blanks.

TAX PAYER:
A man who has the government on the payroll.
A person who works mostly for the government.
Paytriot.

TAXES:
A southern state.
The fine you have to pay for doing okay.

TAXI:
A vehicle that always seems to dissolve in the rain.

TAXI DRIVER:
A man who. .
. . drives away customers.
. . goes through life just missing everything.
. . is always picking up strange women.
. . runs into many interesting people.

TAXIDERMIST:

A man who can mount any animal except a horse.

A man who knows his stuff.

Stuff guy.

TAXIMETER:

A device showing how fast you are not getting there.

TEA:

Blonde coffee.

Blonde water.

TEACHER REPLACEMENT:

Substitutor.

TEACHERS:

People who are trying to get attention.

TEARS:

Headwater.

Glum drops.

The world's greatest water power.

TEEN-AGE:

The time between pigtails and cocktails.

TEEN-AGERS:

People who express a burning drive to be different by dressing exactly alike.

Youngsters who regard home as a drive-in where Pop pays for the hamburgers.

TEETH:

A painful object. If not coming in, when going out.

TELEGRIM:

The sad news.

TELEPHONE:

A chatter box.

An inconvenient convenience.

An instrument that picks up all the dirt.

An invention that causes the most talk.

An object that will always ring when the only person in the house is taking a bath.

TELEPHONE BILL:

Gab fare.

TELEPHONE BOOK:

A list of lonely people.

TELEPHONE GIRL:

A call girl.

A girl who has always has rings in her ears.
TELESCOPE:
A stare case.
TELEVISION:
A device that enables you to see static and hear it.
A device that permits people who haven't anything to do to watch people who can't do anything.
A dim view of life.
A juke box with commercials.
A little box that throws off light without illumination.
A sight for sore eyes.
A watching machine.
Radio fluroscoped.
Radio with eyestrain.
Smog with knobs.
The longest amateur night in history.
The triumph of machinery over people.
Where old pictures go when they fade away.
TEMPER:
A thing that improves the longer you keep it.
Something you lose when you get angry.
The latest rage.
The only thing you can lose and still have.
What you sometimes lose but always find again.
TEMPORARY TAX:
Something as temporary as a permanent wave is permanent.
TENANTS:
One more than nine ants.
TENNIS:
A game in which you settle in court.
Five times two.
TESTAMONIAL DINNER:
A place where you eat chicken and hear baloney.
TEXAS:
A place where men are men and smell like horses.
THANKS:
Something we often return but never borrow.
THANKSGIVING:

A time when we should count our blessing and ignore calories.

THERMOMETER:

An instrument that always has its ups and downs.

An instrument that often falls but never breaks.

An instrument that should be bought in the winter because it is much higher in the summer.

THIEF:

A person who finds things before they get lost.

THIRSTY PHYSICIAN:

Dry dock.

THIRTEEN:

An unlucky number if you only have food enough for twelve.

THIRTY:

A nice age for a woman especially if she is forty.

THOUGHT:

Selected prejudices.

THROAT DOCTOR:

A hoarse doctor.

THUNDER:

Noisy cloud.

THUNDERSTORM:

A flush of lighting.

A loud cloud.

TIGHTWAD:

A man who always sits with his back to the check.

A man with one-way pockets.

TIME:

Always stands still for a woman of thirty.

Something that's either marching on or running out.

Stuff that when you're late for an appointment you're not on.

The only thing that doesn't fly when you try to kill it.

The space between paydays.

TIPS:

Wages we pay other people's hired help.

TITIAN:

The color a poor red-haired girl becomes as soon as her father strikes oil.

189

TOASTMASTER:
An expert on making toast.

A gentleman who introduces a gentleman who needs no introduction.

A man who eats meals he doesn't like, tells stories he doesn't remember to people who have heard it before.

TOBACCO:
Lettuce with a suntan.

TOES:
What a man must be up on it he doesn't want to be down at his heels.

TOMORROW:
The best time to get married.

The day you go on a diet.

TONGUE TWISTER:
A phrase that gets your tongue all tongueled up.

TOOTHACHE:
A pain that drives you to extraction.

TOP SECRET:
A custom-built wig.

TORPEDO:
Sea shell.

TOUPEE:
A breath of fresh hair.

A convertible top.

A false hood.

Instant hair.

Top secret.

TOWEL:
The dirtier it is the cleaner the face.

The only thing that gets wet when it dries.

TOWN:
A small town is a town where. .

. . a fellow with a black eye doesn't have to explain to people, they know.

. . a first aid kit is their medical center.

. . a man is never too busy to tell you how busy he is.

. . a person with a private phone is anti-social.

. . a 2-story house is declared a sky-scraper.

.. a woman will always reach for a chair when answering the telephone.
.. an automatic dishwasher is not bought but married.
.. downtown is right across the street.
.. during a boxing match both fighters have to sit in the same corner.
.. everybody knows the trouble you have seen.
.. everybody knows whose check is good and whose wife isn't.
.. for excitement they go downtown to watch the trains go by.
.. for excitement they go to the A&P and watch them put the awning down.
.. for excitement they go to the airport and look at luggage.
.. for excitement they go to the bakery to smell bread.
.. for excitement they go to the barbecue stand and watch the chicken revolve.
.. for excitement they go to the only hotel and listen to the clerk hitting the desk bell.
.. for excitement they go to the reservoir to see the level drop.
.. for excitement they go to the store and try on gloves.
.. for excitement they open up umbrellas.
.. for excitement they used to watch Alka-Seltzer fizz.
.. for excitement they watch the daily express truck go by.
.. Howard Johnson has only one flavor.
.. if they have a power failure at 10 p.m. nobody will notice it.
.. if you don't hear about it in the general store it didn't happen.
.. if you don't know what's going on, nothing is.
.. if you see a girl dining with a man old enough to be her father he is.
.. .if you turn around once you have seen the place twice.
.. Medicare is known as Minicare.
.. one alarm clock wakes up everybody.
.. only the General store has a telephone.

.. people buy a newspaper only to verify what they heard earlier over the phone.

.. people go to church on Sunday just to see who didn't.

.. people go to the station just to make believe they are leaving.

.. people wonder how you ever got as far as you did.

.. the all night diner closes at 7 p.m.

.. the barber-shop quartet consists of three girls.

.. the baseball team has only four players.

.. the city limit signs are back to back.

.. the cop hides behind the billboard in the next town.

.. the daily paper has only one page.

.. the fire department is a fire extinguisher.

.. the fire department uses a Volkswagen as a fire truck.

.. the fire mascot is a parakeet.

.. the firemen make no housecalls.

.. the highlight of the cultural season is the arrival of a circus.

.. the local paper prints the comic strips on the front page.

.. the main road goes through a car-wash.

.. the most exciting story is the weather report.

.. the news gets around before the newspaper does.

.. the night club closes at 9 p.m.

.. the only place open all night is the mailbox.

.. the only thing that goes out after 10 p.m. is the light.

.. the only thing you can do evenings is go to sleep.

.. the picture postcards show scenes from another town.

.. the phone book has only one page.

.. the police have an unlisted phone number.

.. the post office is the mail box.

.. the postmaster knows more than the schoolmaster.

.. the real news comes over the fence, not over the radio.

.. the Sunday paper can be lifted with one hand.

.. the telephone has only one fingerhole.

.. the town cryer has to whisper after 6 p.m.

.. the town drunk had to leave because he hates to drink alone.

.. the water reservoir is a Dixie cup.

. . the wedding of the month was an elopement from another town.

. . the whole police force can ride on a bicycle.

. . the ZIP code is a decimal.

. . there is no place to go where you shouldn't.

. . there is nothing doing every minute.

. . they are not trying to raise money for an airport.

. . they are proud of a traffic jam.

. . they cancelled the 9 p.m. curfew because it was waking everybody up.

. . they closed the school when the teacher got sick.

. . they eat the midnight snack at 8 p.m.

. . they fired the dogcatcher after he got the dog.

. . they had to cancel the 11 o'clock news because there wasn't any.

. . they had to close the library because someone took the book out.

. . they had to close the zoo, because the duck died.

. . they had to extend the town limits to have enough room for a phone booth.

. . they had to widen the street to put a white line down the middle.

. . they have "COME AGAIN" painted on the back of the "WELCOME" sign.

. . they have no hotel, just a sleeping couch at the bus stop.

. . they have no jail. If punished you have to stand in the corner for a week.

. . they have no sanitation department. A woman comes in twice a week to clean up.

. . they had to call off the night ballgame when the bulb burned out.

. . they hired a traffic cop and then went out to get some traffic.

. . they ring in the New Year at 7 p.m.

. . they say Good Night at four in the afternoon.

. . they shut off the only traffic light at 4 p.m.

. . they start the late, late show at 7:30 p.m.

. . they use a pencil for a computer.

.. when they have a parade there is nobody left to watch it.

.. when you use your electric razor the street lights dim.

.. you can finish the Sunday paper at breakfast.

.. you must have the exact change to get on the airplane.

.. you need a candle to read the electric meter.

TOWING COMPANY:

Crash collector.

TRADE SECRETS:

What women do.

TRAFFIC:

Too many people in too many cars in too much of a hurry going in too many directions.

When you sit in your car and watch pedestrians go by.

TRAFFIC COURT:

Hall of blame.

TRAFFIC LAWS:

Heed aches.

TRAFFIC LIGHT:

A little green light that changes to red as your car approaches.

A place where the speedy and the slow car meet.

A trick to get pedestrians in the middle of the street.

TRAGEDY:

A bride without a can opener.

TRAILER:

A vehicle that gives you a place to live, while you're looking for a place to park.

TRAIN:

The only thing whose tracks you can see even before it has passed.

TRAIN ANNOUNCER:

The most misunderstood man.

TRAITOR:

A California physician who prescribes a change of climate.

TRAMP STEAMER:

Bum voyage.

TRANQUILIZER:

A pill that calms you down, so that instead of making a hasty mistake, you will make a calculated blunder.

TRANSISTOR RADIO:
A small case attached to a teen-ager.

TRAVEL FOLDER:
A trip tease.

TRAVEL OFFICE:
Roam service.

TRAVELER:
One who usually returns with brag and baggage.

TRAVELLING SALESMAN:
A man who comes and goes.
A man who wishes he had as much fun on the road as his wife thinks he does.

TREE:
Something that stands in the same place for years and then suddenly jumps in front of a car.

TRIPLETS:
A pair with a spare.

TRIUMFANT:
Happy to have a baby.

TRIVIAL PURSUIT:
Quizzical fitness.

TROMBONIST:
A man who is always blowing his own horn.
A man who succeeds by letting things slide.

TROUBLE:
The easiest thing in the world to borrow.
The only thing children give parents plenty of.
The only thing many are looking for but nobody wants.

TROUSERS:
An outer garment, singular on the top and plural at the bottom.

TRUANT:
Uncle's real wife.

TRUTHFUL PERSON:
One who doesn't have to remember what he said.

TUMOR:
An extra pair.

TUNA:

A man who fixes pianos.

TUNAFISH:
A fish in a can that comes out when unexpected company comes.

TUNNEL:
An upside down bridge.

TV:
Furniture that talks.

TV CENSOR:
Beeping Tom,

TV COMMERCIAL:
Those brief moments when you pay attention to your wife and kidneys.

TV DINNER:
Chicken a la foil.

TV-MOVIE:
A happy ending preceeded by a sad commercial.

TWICE:
Once more.

UDDER:
A faucet on a cow.

ULCER:
Something that's eating you.

UMBRELLA:
A portable roof.
The only thing some people put away for a rainy day.

UMPIRE:
A man who is no jeweler but a high authority on diamonds.
What a baseball player becomes after he loses his eyesight.

UNABRIDGED:
A river you have to wade across.

UNAWARE:
What you put on first and take off last.

UNDER-RATE:
Seven.

UNDER SEPARATE COVER:
Twin beds.

UNDERPASS:

Upside-down bridge.

UNDERTAKER:
A believer in pay-as-you-go.

UNDERWEAR:
Something that creeps up on you.

UNKEMPT SCULPTOR:
Dirty chiseler.

UNIVERSITY:
A fountain of knowledge where students come to drink.
A mental reservation.

UNTOLD WEALTH:
What you don't put down on your income tax return.

UNTOUCHABLE:
People you can't borrow money from.
The guest towel in the bathroom.

UPPER BERTH:
Where you rise to retire and get down to get up.

UPPER CRUST:
A lot of crumbs held together by dough.

UP-TO-DATE HOUSE:
One with wall-to-wall carpeting, wall-to-wall windows, and back-to-back financing.

URINE:
Opposite from you're out.

URN:
Making money working.

USED CAR:
A car in first crash condition.

USHER:
A theatrical leading man.
One who has a leading role in the theater.

USHERETTE:
A girl who gets paid for putting a man in his place.
A girl who walks down the aisle with you and then leaves you cold.

UTOPIA:
A place, if people went there, it wouldn't be Utopia.

V:
The center of gravity.

VACATION:

A brief relief without the chief.

A holiday from everything but expenses.

A long awaited rest, except for the pocketbook.

A period during which people find out where to stay away from next year.

A period of travel and relaxation when you take twice the clothes and half the money you need.

A period which your boss tells you when to take and your wife tells you where to go.

A time when a man stops doing what his boss wants and starts doing what his wife wants.

A time when you get a sunburn at premium prices.

A way to get into the pink by going into the red.

After a couple of weeks of it you feel good enough to go back to work and poor enough that you have to.

The bigger the summer vacation, the harder the fall.

The shortest distance between two paydays.

Two weeks of playing followed by fifty weeks of paying.

Two weeks on the sand after fifty weeks on the rocks.

What mothers get when children go to camp.

What you need just right after you had one.

What you take when you can't take what you have been taking.

What your wife has to take to recover from exhaustion of packing for it.

VACATION FOLDER:

A trip tease.

VACUUM:

An empty space with nothing around it.

VACUUM CLEANER:

A broom with a stomach.

Sonic broom.

VAMPIRE'S SON:

A bat boy.

VANGUARD:

A man who guards a truck.

VATICAN USHER:

A Papal People Seater.

VAULTS:

A slow dance like the Merry Widow Vaults.

VEGETABLE:
A substance used to balance a child's plate while it's being carried to and from the table.

VEGETABLE PATCH:
Garden of eatin'.

VEGETABLE SALAD:
Condensed garden.

VEGETARIAN:
One who won't eat anything that moves.

VELOCITY:
The speed a person puts a hot plate down with.

VENETIAN BLINDS:
A thing with a shady reputation.

VENTRILOQUIST:
A man who talks to himself for a living.

VERY:
More than some but less than most.

VETERINARIAN:
A doctor who makes horse calls.
A doctor who treats his patients like dogs.

VETERINARIAN WITH LARYNGITIS:
A hoarse doctor.

VINE:
Vot you drink ven you haf no whiskey.

VIOLATOR:
A man who plays the viola.

VIOLINIST:
A musician who always starts from scratch.

VIRGIN FOREST:
A place where the hand of man has never set foot.

VIRUS:
What people who can't spell pneumonia get.

VISION:
What people think you have when you guess correctly.

VITAMIN:
A modern substitute for food.
What you do when your guests come to visit.

VODKA:
Stuff that's odorless, colorless and tasteless but leaves you senseless.

VOLCANO:
A mountain that blew its top.
A mountain with a fireplace inside.
A mountain with hiccups.
A mountain with high blood pressure.
A sick mountain.

VOWELS:
Something people take before they get married.

WAFFLE:
A batter cake with non-skid tread.
Non-skid pancake.

WAGE DATA:
Income poop.

WAIST MEASUREMENT:
Pouch line.

WAITER:
A man who believes money grows on trays.
A man who finally comes to him who waits.
A menu with back talk.

WALKIE TALKIE:
Two girls down the street.
The opposite of Sittie-stillie.

WALKING:
A primitive method of locomotion achieved by putting
one foot in front of the other.

WALLET:
A device that permits you to lose all your valuables at
the same time.

WALLFLOWER:
A girl who returns home with the same lipstick on her
lips she started out with.
A girl who wears a sweater to keep herself warm.

WARD HEALER:
A hospital physician.

WASHINGTON:
The only place in the world where sound travels faster
than light.

WASHINGTON BRIDGE AT RUSH HOUR:
The Star-Spangled Spanner.

WASHINGTON COMMITTEE:

The unwilling recruited from the unfit to perform the unnecessary.

WATCH REPAIRMAN:
A man who always has time on his hands.
A tic doc.

WATER:
A clear liquid that turns dark when you put your hands in.
A drink with less calories than a diet cola.
A liquid that always freezes with the slippery side up.
A liquid that can both float and sink a ship.
Ice at ease.
100-proof humidity.
Stuff that floats under bridges.
Stuff that makes a very good sidewalk, when mixed with sand and cement.
The stuff that waiters bring you sometimes.
Warm ice.
What some people drink when they run out of beer.

WATER COOLER:
A thirst-aid kit.

WATER TOWER:
A small town's skyline.

WATERFALL:
A drop of water.

WATERMELON:
A fruit you can eat, drink and wash your face at the same time.

WEATHERMAN:
A fellow who can look in a girls's eye and can tell whether.

WEDDING:
A ceremony at which a man loses complete control of himself.
A fine way for two people to get married.
A public announcement of a private intention.
What you have to have first before you can get a divorce.

WEDDING RING:
A vicious circle.

The smallest handcuff in the world.

WEDDING VEIL:
Something worn by the bride to hide her smile of triumph.

WELL-BRED MAN:
A man who can insult another person in public and make it sound like brilliant conversation.

WELL DIGGER:
A man who begins on top and works his way down.

WEST:
A place where men are men and women love it.

WESTERN UNION:
Message parlors.

WESTERN SANDWICH:
Two slices of bread with wide open spaces in between.

WETHER:
A bad spell of weather.

WHEAT:
Blond grain.

WHISKEY:
A beverage that makes friends warm.

A drink that makes you well when you are sick and makes you sick when you are well.

A drink that may shorten your life, but you'll see twice as much in half the time.

A drink that takes away the taste of water.

Instant courage.

Nose paint.

The best key for unlocking the tongue.

Trouble put up in liquid form.

WHITE HOUSE:
Honorable mansion.

WIDOW:
A woman who always knows where her husband is.

WIDOWER:
The only man who has an angel for a wife.

WIFE:
A woman who. .

. . can dish it out but can't cook.

. . dresses to kill and cooks the same way.

. . generally speaking, is generally speaking.

. . has a made up face, serves heated-up dinners, charges up bills, and has a fed-up husband.

. . has never anything to wear and six closets to keep it in.

. . is a dish-jockey.

. . is a former sweetheart.

. . is a husband's bitter half.

. . is a thing of beauty and a jaw forever.

. . is a Walkie-Talkie.

. . is dear to her husband before marriage and even more expensive after.

. . is most attached to a man.

. . is one of the chief obstacles to a happy marriage.

. . is something a man can't get along with or without.

. . is something a man marries.

. . is the contrary sex.

. . plays bridge, tennis, gold, and dumb.

. . reaches for a chair when answering the telephone.

. . sits up with you when you are sick and puts up with you when you are not.

. . sticks with her husband through all the troubles he would never have if he hadn't married her in the first place.

. . wants a roof over her head and a husband under her thumb.

. . when you hear somebody in the kitchen tidying up, it's her mother.

. . would rather mend your ways than your socks.

WIFE OF A DUKE:

A ducky.

WIFE STEALER:

Mate lifter.

WIG:

A convertible top.

False hood.

Wash and wear hair.

WIG FITTING:

Tress rehearsal.

WIGGLE:

A baby's toupee.

WILL:

A dead give-away.

WILL POWER:

The ability to eat only one salted peanut.

WIND:

Air in a rush.

Weather on the go.

WINDOW:

A looking-out glass.

A something that if you throw stuff through it and it's not open there's a big crash.

An invention that enables people to look through brick walls.

WINDOW DRESSER:

A girl who never pulls down the shade.

WINDOW SCREEN:

A device for keeping flies in the house.

WINDOW SHOPPER:

A store gazer.

An eye browser.

WINE:

Borscht with a kick in it.

Good-natured alcohol.

High octane grape juice.

Liquid grapes.

WINK:

An optical allusion.

WINOS:

The grape society.

WINTER:

A season that's so cold that even the wind howls about it.

The season when you keep the house so hot as it was in the summer when you complained about it.

The time when you discover you just got a case of frostbite on top of your Florida sunburn.

The time when you spend one day skiing and ten days in the hospital.

The time your neighbor returns the bottle of suntan lotion and borrows some cough medicine.

WISE HUSBAND:
 One who buys his wife such fine chinaware she doesn't
 trust him to wash the dishes.
WISE PARENTS:
 People who learn to sleep when the baby isn't looking.
WISECRACKER:
 A smart cookie.
 Flips quips.
WIT:
 Wisdom in tidbits.
WITCH:
 A creepy-time gal.
WOLF:
 A man who. .
 . . always aims to squeeze.
 . . believes in life, liberty and the happiness of pursuit.
 . . has a girl on his knees without having her on his hands.
 . . gives women the best leers of his life.
 . . is a big dame hunter.
 . . is a hit-and-run lover.
 . . knows all the ankles.
 . . pays attention without intention.
 . . spends all his time dame dreaming.
 . . thinks the world owes him a loving.
 . . whistles at his work.
 . . to whom a girl whispers sweet nothing doing.
WOMAN:
A person who. .
 . . can skin a wolf and get a mink.
 . . can stay longer on the phone than on a diet.
 . . dresses for men's eyes and for women's eyebrows.
 . . generally speaking, is generally speaking.
 . . goes to a football game to look for mink coats.
 . . is a girl with wrinkles.
 . . is a member of the contrary sex.
 . . is a member of the speaker sex.
 . . is a member of the weeper sex.
 . . is a thing of beauty and a jaw forever.
 . . is always thinking it takes two to keep a secret.

. . is God's second mistake.

. . is most attached to men.

. . is something a man can't get along with or without.

. . is the female of the speeches.

. . is the kind of problem men like to wrestle with.

. . is the so called tender gender.

. . needs shoes larger inside than outside.

. . remains in the twenties between teen-age and middle-age.

. . sometimes get so tired she can't hardly keep her mouth open.

. . will spend $40 on a slip and be annoyed if it shows.

WOMAN DRIVER:

A driver who believes one bad turn deserves another.

A driver who gets caught in a traffic jam that wouldn't have happened if she wasn't there.

A fender bender.

WOMAN GOLFER:

Reckless driver.

WOMAN GOSSIP:

A gab bag.

WOMEN'S DRESS SHOP:

A wear-house.

WOMAN'S FASHION:

Those things that go in one year and out the other.

WOMAN'S HANDBAG:

Steamer trunk.

WOMAN'S INTUITION:

A suspicion that turns out to be true.

WOMAN'S PURSE:

A velvet-lined junkyard.

WOMAN'S TEA:

A place where females go to giggle, gab, gobble and git.

WOMAN'S TEARS:

The most efficient water power in the world.

WOMAN'S TENNIS MATCH:

Volley of the bells.

WOMAN'S TONGUE:

Something that does not go without saying.

WORD:

Something you must keep after giving it to another.

WORM:

A caterpillar that played strip poker and lost.

WORRIES:

Condition produced by lack of money.

WORRY:

Interest we pay on trouble before it is due.

WORK:

An unpopular way of making money.

Something, if a man is happy at, he whistles while he.

The best way to kill time.

WORKING HOURS:

Daylight slaving time.

WRESTLING:

A person who bends over backwards to make a living.

A struggling actor.

WRINKLES:

Head lines.

Something that if a prune doesn't have it it's a plum.

What a woman gets by worrying about her complexion.

Yesterday's dimples.

XEROX MACHINE:

Copycat.

X-RAY:

A preview of coming extraction.

Bellyvision.

The real inside dope.

XPHOBIA:

Fear of words beginning with X.

YACHT:

A floating debt.

YAWN:

The only time some married men ever get to open their mouth.

YEARN:

What a man does for a woman before marriage.

YELLOW:

What people are when they tell white lies.

YES:

The answer to any question the boss asks.

YESMAN:
A man who sees aye to aye with his boss.

YHTAPME:
Empathy spelled backwards.

YO:
A broken yo-yo.

YOKEL:
The yellow part of an eggle.

YOUTHFUL FIGURE:
What you get when you ask a woman her age.

YOUTH FASHION:
Weirdrobe.

ZEBRA:
A black horse with venetian blinds.

A donkey who sat on a park bench before the paint was dry.

A horse behind bars.

A horse in sport clothes.

A horse wearing slipcovers.

A horse whose mother was frightened by an awning.

A sport model donkey.

Either a light animal with dark stripes or a dark animal with white stripes.

Horses who can't get their pajamas off.

What ze French women wear.

ZERO:
Just a word for nothing.

Something that's nothing at all.

ZITHER:
A dehydrated harp.

A lap harp.

ZOO:
A place where animals can be kept safe behind bars to study people.

A place where parents take their children and then forget to leave them there.

Where the deer and antelope stay.

ZWIEBACK:
A toast that's never drunk.

ZZ:
Sound made by sleeping people.

Rhyming Dictionary

A la carte; MEAL DEAL.
A person waiting for the doctor; PATIENT PATIENT.
Aquire antelope; NEW GNU.
African beat-music instrument; CONGO BONGO.
After-dark bout; NIGHT FIGHT.
Airconditioned school; COOL SCHOOL.
Air of superiority; WISE GUISE.
Airline stewardess; PLANE JANE.
Airport; AVIATION STATION.
Airport runway; PLANE LANE.
Alcohol ticket; LIQUOR STICKER.
Almanac; ANNUAL MANUAL.
All-right chimp; HUNKY MONKEY.
Altitude record holder; HIGHER FLIER.
Amiable bird; PLEASANT PHEASANT.
Amusing rabbit; FUNNY BUNNY.
An antler animal's dessert; MOOSE MOUSSE.
Anesthesia; AROMA COMA.
Angry boy; MAD LAD.
Angry father; MAD DAD.
Animal feet stop; PAWS PAUSE.
Animal story; CREATURE FEATURE.
Ant living in carpet; RUG BUG.
Apehouse; GORILLA VILLA.

Appendage story; TAIL TALE.
Applause; CHEERFUL EARFUL.
Arithmetic trail; MATH PATH.
Arrogant horse rider; COCKY JOCKEY.
Arthritis; HINGES TWINGES.
Art store compensation; GALLERY SALARY.
Aviator; FLY GUY.
A.W.O.L.; ROOKIE HOOKY.
Baby calf; NEW MOO.
Baby with fever; HOTSY-TOTSY.
Baby nursery; WET SET.
Baby sitter; YELPER HELPER.
Baby's cow answer to a joke; CALF LAUGH.
Bad boy; WILD CHILD.
Bad chicken; FOUL FOWL.
Bad interpretation; MISLEADING READING.
Bad poem; WORSE VERSE.
Bad woman; SHADY LADY.
Bald-headed old crow; SHAVEN RAVEN.
Banana from Cuba; HAVANA BANANA.
Band uniform; TOOT SUIT.
Bangs on fire; FRINGE SINGE.
Bar in a cave; CAVERN TAVERN.
Barbershop; CHOP SHOP.
Barrister at the habor bar; LEGAL SEAGULL.
Basement salesperson; CELLAR SELLER.
Bashful lad; COY BOY.
Bashful snooper; SHY SPY.
Bashful winged insect; SHY FLY.
Baket game; COURT SPORT.
Basketball reporter; DRIBBLER SCRIBBLER.
Beach; SUN FUN.
Beach umbrella; SWELTER SHELTER.
Beatnick plumber; DRIPPY HIPPIE.
Beautiful girl; SLICK CHICK.
Bee kept in a bottle; JUG BUG.
Bee with hay fever; BEEZER WHEEZER.
Beekeeper's income; HONEY MONEY.
Belgian food; BRUSSEL MUSSLES.
Biased craftsman; PARTISAN ARTISAN.

Bicycle; POLLUTION SOLUTION.
Bikini underwear; SCANTY PANTY.
Bird feeder; TWEETER TREATER.
Bird living around cows; DAIRY CANARY.
Birthday gift; PLESANT PRESENT.
Biscuit packer; CRACKER SACKER.
Bleached color; FAINT PAINT.
Blizzard; SNOW WOE.
Blonde bombshell; FOXY DOXEY.
Blood bank; VEIN DRAIN.
Bloody yarn; GORY STORY.
Boat canvas bargains; SAIL SALE.
Boastful illusionist; EGOISTIC MYSTIC.
Boring bird; DULL GULL.
Boxer's no-no; LOW BLOW.
Boy who is afraid; YELLOW FELLOW.
Bragging spirit; GHOST BOAST.
Braver rock; BOLDER BOULDER.
Breakfast fish exporter; KIPPER SHIPPER.
Breakfast food for spirit; GHOSTIES TOASTIES.
Brief visit; SMALL CALL.
Bug's trousers; ANT'S PANTS.
Bumpy racetrack; COARSE COURSE.
Bunny's daily routine; RABBIT HABIT.
Burgundy; FINE WINE.
Burning car wheel; TIRE FIRE.
Business lunch; MEAL DEAL.
Busy head of school; KEEN DEAN.
Cable railway up a precipice; PERPENDICULAR FU-
    NICULAR.
Caged bird who has fallen into a swamp; SLUDGY
    BUDGIE.
Candy bar; SWEET TREAT.
Car-accident lawyer; FENDER BENDER DEFENDER.
Car purchase; WHEEL DEAL.
Car sakesman; WHEELER DEALER.
Careless driver; FENDER BENDER.
Cartons for anklets; SOX BOX.
Carpenter; HAMMER SLAMMER.
Cat who tells funny stories; WITTY KITTY.

Cattle rustler; BEEF THIEF.
Cautious spirit; WARY FAIRY.
Changing the church platform; ALTER ALTAR.
Cheap germ; INFERIOR BACTERIA.
Checkers; TAME GAME.
Check-out counter forman; CHECKER CHECKER.
Cheerful father; GLAD DAD.
Cheese grater; CHEDDAR SHREDDER.
Chef who can't hear; DEAF CHEF.
Chicken purchaser; FRYER BUYER.
Childbirth at the northpole; SHIVERY DELIVERY.
Children's playground; TOT LOT.
Child's bicycle; TOT ROD.
Choosy girl; FUSSY HUSSY.
Circular hill; ROUND MOUND.
Clean navy; NEAT FLEET.
Cleaned up; LESS MESS.
Clever ploy; SLICK TRICK.
Clever song; WITTY DITTY.
Closet; BROOM ROOM.
Cocktail sausage; TEENY WEENY.
Color of the sky; BLUE HUE.
Comedy writer; LAUGHTER DRAFTER.
Compliment; CHEERFUL EARFUL.
Conceited blood channel; VAIN VEIN.
Contour chair; SLOUCH COUCH.
Convict's meal; SINNER DINNER.
Cordless phone; WALKIE TALKIE.
Corn sheller; COB JOB.
Corny labyrinth; MAIZE MAZE.
Correct ceremony; PROPER STOPPER.
Corridor of an island; ISLE AISLE.
Costly lager; DEAR BEER.
Courageous squire; BRAVE KNAVE.
Coward; YELLOW FELLOW.
Crazy Chinese food; SCREWY CHOP SUEY.
Crazy flower; CRAZY DAISY.
Criminal shellfish; MOBSTER LOBSTER.
Crooked little finger; KINKY PINKY.
Cruise; SHIP TRIP.

Cruel ruler; MEAN QUEEN.
Crusader's torch; KNIGHT LIGHT.
Cry from large animal; WHALE WAIL.
Cuban fruit; HAVANA BANANA.
Cute kitten; PRETTY KITTY.
Dancehall bouncer; EAGER HEAVER.
Darning cotton of a certain color; RED THREAD.
Date; SWEET MEET.
Dejected boy; SAD LAD.
Delighted father; HAPPY PAPPY.
Departed spouse; LATE MATE.
Deputy; PARTIAL MARSHAL.
Dessert; EAT TREAT.
Dessert cart; CALORIE GALLERY.
Dill that keeps changing color; FICKLE PICKLE.
Disappearing virus; FLU FLEW.
Dog conversation; BOWWOW POWWOW.
Dog fight; BOW ROW.
Dog house; MUTT HUT.
Dog show; OODLES OF POODLES.
Dod's kiss; POOCH SMOOCH.
Double stitch; SEW-SEW.
Double sword fight; DUAL DUEL.
Dread; SHEER FEAR.
Drinking fountain in the Catskills; MOUNTAIN
     FOUNTAIN.
Drooler; DRIP LIP.
Drunkard; WHISKEY FRISKY.
Drunkard on a hot day; HOT SOT.
Drunken bug; PIE-EYE FLY.
Dumb cherub; STUPID CUPID.
Dumb seabird; DULL GULL.
Eager rooster; HEN YEN.
Earthquake; CHASM SPASM. ACRE SHAKER.
11 a.m.; SOON NOON.
Election result; POLL TOLL.
Embarrassed citizen of Moscow: BLUSHIN' RUSSIAN.
English horn teacher; TUDOR TOOTER TUTOR.
Entire burrow; WHOLE HOLE.
Escaped fowl; LOOSE GOOSE.

213

Escaped honey-maker; FREE BEE.
Ether; AROMA COMA.
Eve; MADAM ADAM.
Eve's bikini; EVE'S LEAVES.
Eve's mini; FIG RIG.
Exotic food at a banquet; RARE FARE.
Extented carol; LONG SONG.
Eye doctor; WINKER TINKER.
Fake horse; PHONEY PONY.
Fake salami; PHONEY BALONEY.
Fast food place; ECONOMY GASTRONOMY.
Fast duck; QUICK QUACK.
Fast taste of ice cream; QUICK LICK.
Fast tricycle; TROT ROD.
Fat ape; CHUNKY MONKEY.
Fat cat; FLABBY TABBY.
Fat fish; STOUT TROUT.
Fat husband; CHUBBY HUBBY.
Fat man; WHALE MALE.
Father who is hitting people; SLAP-HAPPY PAPPY.
Favorite dessert; YELLOW JELLOW.
Fearful man quivering; COWARD COWERED.
Female deer sleeping; DOES DOZE.
Famale monarch; TEEN QUEEN.
Female press agent; PITCH WITCH.
Female private eye; SLICK CHICK DICK.
Female sheep utilize; EWES USE.
Feverish baby; HOT TOT.
Fig leaf. TEENY BIKINI.
Fighting apes; GORILLA GUERILLA.
Final explosion; LAST BLAST.
Fine furniture; GOOD WOOD.
Fine janitor; SUPER SUPER.
Fine coed dance; SMARTY PARTY.
Fireproof container; SAFE SAFE.
First bikini; EVE'S LEAVES.
Fisherman's annual; HOOK BOOK.
Fishing rod for catching gophers; MOLE POLE.
Five-cent cucumber; NICKLE PICKLE.
Flashy feline; FAT CAT.

Flattery; EARFUL CHEERFUL.
Flirtation; DAME GAME.
Flob house. CHEAP SLEEP.
Flock listened; HERD HEARD.
Floppy dirigible; LIMB BLIMP.
Flue epidemic; VIRAL SPIRAL.
Fluff; LIP SLIP.
Fog information; SOUP POOP.
Foggy light; DAMP LAMP.
Food taster wages; CALORIE SALARY.
Foolish horse; SILLY FILLY.
Forbidden music group; BANNED BAND.
Fortunate water bird; LUCKY DUCKY.
Free dinner; EAT TREAT.
Fresh young girl; SASSY LASSIE.
Fresh vegetable; GREEN BEAN.
Friendly dog; SMOOCHIE POOCHIE.
Frighten man; PALE MALE.
Frigid Christmas; COOL YULE.
Frowsy apartment; SAD PAD.
Frozen snow on a bike; BICYCLE ICICLE.
Frozen wrench; COOL TOOL.
Fun kid; JOY BOY.
Funeral in Helsinki; FINNISH FINNISH.
Funny joke; BEST JEST.
Funny rhyme; WITTY DITTY.
Funny story about the yellow egg part; YOLK JOKE.
Fur thief; STOLE STOLE.
Funny show; GAY PLAY.
Gardenhose; FAKE SNAKE.
Gasoline; MOTION LOTION.
Get-together at noon; LUNCH BUNCH.
Giant fish selling for half price; WHALE SALE.
Girl friend; GAL PAL.
Glass agony; PANE PAIN.
Glue-covered man named Richard; STICKY RICKY.
Goat that made you laugh; SILLY BILLY.
Goldfish; WET PET.
Golf expenses; TEE FEE.
Good news; CHEERFUL EARFUL.

Good posture; FINE SPINE.
Goosefarm magazine; GOOSE NEWS.
Gory girl; BLOODY BUDDY.
Gossip; CHEAT CHAT. PEDDLING MEDDLING.
    RETAIL DETAIL.
Grandma; MOTHER'S MOTHER.
Grieving at dawn; MORNING MOURNING.
Grouchy taxi driver; CRABBY CABBY.
Group of feathered animals; BIRD HERD.
Gruesome tale; GORY STORY.
Half-dozen cops; SIX DICKS.
Hall closet; BROOM ROOM.
Hamburger; FAKE STEAK.
Happy boy; GLAD LAD.
Happy parrot; JOLLY POLLY.
Haunted spectre of a departed chicken; PHANTOM
    BANTAM.
Haunted wigwam; CREEPY TEEPEE.
Hay fever; FLOWER POWER.
Headache. BRAIN PAIN. ATTIC STATIC.
Healthy dog; SOUND HOUND.
Heavy metal cot; LEAD BED.
Highly polished Irish Lebrechaun; CHROME GNOME.
Hip simpleton; COOL FOOL.
Hobo in the rain; DAMP TRAMP.
Hold-up man in a meatmarket; BEEF THIEF.
Horrible bear; GRISLY GRIZZLY.
Horseman of the year; COCKEY JOCKEY.
Humorous rabbit; FUNNY BUNNY.
Hurled royal chair; THROWN THRONE.
Icicle; WINTER SPLINTER.
Icy remark; FROZE POSE.
Imitation pond; FAKE LAKE.
Imitation sausage; PHONEY BOLONEY.
Inexpensive Indian tent; CHEEPIE TEEPEE.
Inexperienced monarch; GREEN QUEEN.
Irritable supervisor; CROSS BOSS.
Insane embrace; BUG HUG.
Insect relative; ANT AUNT.
Irene; DAME NAME.

Jail fence; TALL WALL.
Jitterbug fowl; JERKY TURKEY.
Joy; SHEER CHEER.
Jungle movie; CREATURE FEATURE.
Kid's bedtime; PAJAMA DRAMA.
Large archeologist; BIGGER DIGGER.
Large chimp; HUNKY MONKEY.
Last car of an Elk train; MOOSE CABOOSE.
Late air journey; NIGHT FLIGHT.
Leather; DRIED HIDE.
Legal loophole; LAW FLAW.
Levy on nails; TACKS TAX.
Librarian; READER FEEDER.
Light-colored bucket; PALE PAIL.
Likeable ground bird; PLEASANT PHEASANT.
Limerick; WITTY DITTY.
Line of fish eggs; ROE ROW.
Little creature in the woods; VIRILE SQUIRREL.
Lively gatherings; HEARTY PARTY.
Lobster desire; FISH DISH WISH.
Lollipop; HANDY CANDY.
Loser of a dog fight; GROGGY DOGGIE.
Love bug; DESIROUS VIRUS.
Lumber yard; BOARD HOARD.
Machine oil; MOTION LOTION.
Mad about theater; DRAMATIC FANATIC.
Magazine thief; BOOK CROOK.
Magic; HOCUS POCUS. QUICK TRICK.
Mahagony; GOOD WOOD.
Mailed penny; SENT CENT.
Main code of conduct; PRINCIPAL PRINCIPLE.
Make-believe pain; FAKE ACHE.
Male float; BOY BUOY.
Mammogram; BREAST TEST.
Man from Karachi doing fakir tricks; UNCANNY PAKI-
    STANI.
Man living in basement; CELLAR DWELLER.
Man looking for tennis shoes; SNEAKER SEEKER.
Man who boxes cookies; CRACKER PACKER.
Man who cuts hair at seaport; HABOR BARBER.

Man who likes to tie knots; KNOT NUT.
Man who makes NAVY clothes; SAILOR TAILOR.
Man who washes whales; BLUBBER SCRUBBER.
Man who works for free; WORK JERK.
Man tasting candy for a living; FUDGE JUDGE.
Mansion's etiquette; MANOR'S MANNERS.
Maple sugar; SWEET TREAT.
Marathon; FUN RUN. FLEET FEET FEAT.
Marriage proposal; HITCH PITCH.
Masculine postal item; MALE MAIL.
Matrimony; DOUBLE TROUBLE.
Meat dish error; SWISS-STEAK MISTAKE.
Medication drop; PILL SPILL.
Medieval darkness; KNIGHT NIGHT.
Menu; MEAL DEAL.
Messy looking cat; SHABBY TABBY.
Messy sailor; SLOB GOB.
Midget skunk; SHRUNK SKUNK.
Midnight supper; LATE DATE.
Military belly button; NAVAL NAVEL.
Miniature car; BOY TOY.
Missed kiss; LIP SLIP.
Mistake a ghost made; BOO BOO.
Mixed-up girl; CRAZY DAISY.
Moby Dick; PALE WHALE.
Modern art; OODLES OF DOODLES.
Mohair jacket; GOAT COAT.
Monday's ice cream; MONDAY SUNDAE.
Money charged for a teepee; TENT RENT.
Money owed for wager; BET DEBT.
Monkey house; GORILLA VILLA.
More than nine males; TEN MEN.
Moron playing billard; POOL FOOL.
Mosquito's home; PEST NEST.
Mother of a million eggs; FERTILE TURTLE.
Mouth of a cross person; POUT SNOUT.
Multi-story shopping center; TALL MALL.
Mummy that eats cookies in bed; CRUMMY MUMMY.
Naked grizzly; BARE BEAR.
Naked rabbit; BARE HARE.

Necking; PASSION FASHION.
Nerve doctor; TIC DOC.
Network censor; BLEEP CREEP.
New Computer; KEEN MACHINE.
Never ending aria; LONG SONG.
Nice chair; NEAT SEAT.
Nice gift; PLEASANT PRESENT.
Nice hotel room; SWEET SUITE:
Nice pig; FINE SWINE.
Nightshirt; NAP SACK.
Nimble insect; SPRY FLY.
Noisy meeting; RAUCOUS CAUCUS.
Noise people; LOUD CROWD.
Noncommital; BLAND STAND.
Non-sanforized men's underwear; SHRUNK TRUNK.
Nurse's pocketbook; NURSE PURSE.
Nude Indian maiden; RAW SQUAW.
Nudist; BUFF BUFF.
Nymphomaniac; EROTIC NEUROTIC.
Odd fortune teller; QUEER SEER.
Odd market place; BIZARRE BAZAAR.
Old letters; STALE MAIL.
Old musical instrument; MELLOW CELLO.
Old story; STALE TALE.
Old truck; SORRY LORRY.
Old unsolved puzzle; HISTORY MYSTERY.
Out-of-town boy friend; COMMUTER SUITER.
Overjoyed father; HAPPY PAPPY.
Overweight car; HEAVY CHEVY.
Overweight rodent; FAT RAT.
Paid bill; MET DEBT.
Parking problem; SPACE RACE.
Particular kitten; FUSSY PUSSY.
Party in hell; DEVIL REVEL.
Pay TV; TV FEE.
Peep; SNEAK PEEK.
Peeping Tom; PEEK FREAK.
Perfume; SMELL WELL.
Peril of a forest patrolman; RANGER DANGER.

Person who is an eager performer; DRAMATIC FA-NATIC.

Phony cobra; FAKE SNAKE.

Photography; FOCUS POCUS.

Pickpocket; TROUSER BROWSER.

Piece of chocolate dropped on the beach; SANDY CANDY.

Pilot; FLY GUY.

Place where the Mayflower landed; ROCK DOCK.

Place where you study to be a vampire; GHOUL SCHOOL.

Pleasant rodent; NICE MICE.

Pleasure cruise; SHIP TRIP.

Playground; TOT LOT.

Plumber's assistant; DRAINEE TRAINEE.

Poet's hat; SONNET BONNET.

Police commissioner; TOP COP.

Police station; COP STOP.

Policeman's ball; COP HOP.

Policeman's coffe cup; COP CUP.

Polo; SNOBBY HOBBY.

Pond; FAKE LAKE.

Polution free; FAIR AIR.

Poor poetry; WORSE VERSE.

Poor reproduction; SLOPPY COPY.

Portugese worker; BRAZILIAN CIVILIAN.

Postman; MAIL MALE.

Postpone the fur; TABLE SABLE.

Praising a power supply; BATTERY FLATTERY.

Precious buck; DEAR DEER.

Pretend pain; FAKE ACHE.

Pretty clarinet; CUTE FLUTE.

Pretty girl stung; BITTEN KITTEN.

Prisoner's last meal; SINNER DINNER.

Proofreader; BLOOPER SNOOPER.

Psychiatrist; COUCH COACH.

Punk haircut; SHEARED WEIRD.

Puppy's diary; DOG LOG.

Quacker who won the lottery; LUCKY DUCKY.

Rabbit fur; HARE HAIR.

Raspy throated equine; HOARSE HORSE.
Rat-infested bus station; VERMINOUS TERMINUS.
Reason for divorce; HATE MATE.
Recreation area for large fish; SHARK PARK.
Reducing salon; SLIM GYM.
Reform school; BRAT TRAP.
Rendezvous; GREAT DATE.
Rest from putting up a tent; STAKE BREAK.
Revolt; SURPRISING UPRISING.
Ring around the collar; SHIRT DIRT.
Ripped cornet; TORN HORN.
Rodent living indoors; HOUSE MOUSE.
Rodent's mate; MOUSE SPOUSE.
Rodent's rug; RAT MAT.
Romantic cat; SMITTEN KITTEN.
Room for rent; PAD AD.
Rose dipped in vinegar; SOUR FLOWER.
Rotten potato; DUD SPUD.
Rough track; COARSE COURSE.
Royal tiny fish; QUEEN SARDINE.
Rubber skeleton; PHONEY BONEY.
Rude fish; CRASS BASS.
Rude high-school girl; SURLY GIRLY.
Run-down flat; SAD PAD.
Runway; PLANE LANE.
Ruthless combat; CRUEL DUEL.
Sailor's tour; CREW'S CRUISE.
San Francisco street car; CHAIN TRAIN.
Scarecrow; CROP COP.
Seasickness; OCEAN MOTION NOTION.
Seed catalog; KERNEL JOURNAL.
Sermon; PREACHER FEATURE.
Sewer; RAIN DRAIN.
Shaking tummy; JELLY BELLY.
Shellfish colony; OYSTER CLOISTER.
Sherlock Holmes; SUPER SNOOPER.
Ship's paper; CRUISE NEWS.
Shooting gallery; GUN FUN.
Short gag; FUN PUN.
Short Indian leader; BRIEF CHIEF.

Short poem; TERSE VERSE.
Short strong stick; STUB CLUB.
Shy plaything; COY TOY.
Simple aircraft; PLAIN PLANE.
Sizzling skillet; HOT POT.
Skinny Scandinavian; THIN FINN.
Skinny young horse; BONY PONY.
Skunk; NASAL APPRAISAL.
Skywriter's hellow; HIGH HI!
Slave market; MALE SALE.
Sleep; BEST REST.
Slight caprice; FLIMSY WHIMSY.
Slippery razor; SLICK SCHICK.
Skillful stunt with wood; STICK TRICK.
Small sausage; TEENIE WEENIE.
Small stingy insect; WEE BEE.
Small writing; MINIATURE SIGNATURE.
Smart fiancee; BRIGHT BRIDE.
Smart gambler; BETTER BETTOR.
Smiling rabbit; FUNNY BUNNY.
Smoking car-wheel; TIRE FIRE.
Snake charmer; VIPER PIPER.
Sober pillar; SOLEMN COLUMN.
Something shot from a tiny bow; NARROW ARROW.
Song about lettuce and tomatoes; SALAD BALLAD.
Sore loser; BITTER QUITTER.
Special writing paper; STATIONARY STATIONERY.
Speed set by a sprinter. RACE PACE.
Spun globe; WHIRLED WORLD.
Stable story; BARN YARN.
Stick for roasting beef; STEAK STAKE.
Story aboput horses; STABLE TABLE.
Strange whiskers; WEIRD BEARD.
Street walker; SHADY LADY.
Stupid derlict; DUMB BUM.
Stupid mummy; DUMMY MUMMY.
Stupid ruler; DING-A-LING KING.
Stylish gun; MOD ROD.
Sufficient specimen. AMPLE SAMPLE.
Sunburned hand; RAW PAW.

Surfboarding; TIDE RIDE.
Sympathy card; PITY DITTY.
Tact; CONVERSATION CONSERVATION.
Tadpole's diary; FROG LOG.
Talkative parakeet; WORDY BIRDY.
Taller aviator; HIGHER FLYER.
Teapot; METAL KETTLE.
Tea sample; FREE TEA.
Teddy bear; BOY TOY.
The White house; PRESIDENT'S RESIDENCE.
Thinking; BRAIN DRAIN.
Traffic policeman; CAR CZAR.
Transparent nightgown; PANORAMA JAMA.
Timid lecturer; MEEKER SPEAKER.
Trick photography; FOCUS POCUS.
Tricycle; TYKE BIKE. TOT ROD.
Trojan horse. PHONY PONY.
Tuna plate; FISH DISH.
Twins; DOUBLE TROUBLE.
Two good-looking girls; FAIR PAIR.
Two monsters; GRUESOME TWOSOME.
Unattached fowl; LOOSE GOOSE.
Unbroken dish; WHOLE BOWL.
Unheated swimming pool; COOL POOL.
Unruly child; WILD CHILD.
Unsolved puzzle from long time ago; HISTORY
    MYSTERY.
Unsuccessful barter; STALE SALE.
Used-car dealer; WHEELER DEALER.
Vacation; BEST REST.
Venice; PRETTY CITY.
Very cunning blonde bombshell; FOXY DOXEY.
Villianous singer; BASE BASS.
Villianous tramp; FLAGRANT VAGRANT.
Violin quiz; FIDDLE RIDDLE.
Visitor estimated; GUEST GUESSED.
Water pistol; FUN GUN.
Waves; OCEAN MOTION.
Wedding rehearsal; AISLE TRIAL.
Weekend ice cream treat; SUNDAY SUNDAE.

Well-behaved rodents; NICE MICE.
Well-dressed fish; SHARP CARP.
Well-dressed girl; SLICK CHICK.
Well-groomed cartographer; DAPPER MAPPER.
Wet hobo; DAMP TRAMP.
Wet pooch; SOGGIE DOGGIE.
Wet seal; DAMP STAMP.
Wet tadpole; SOGGY FROGGY.
Whale washer; BLUBBER SCRUBBER.
What a foot doctor does; HEALS HEELS.
What the doctor likes; PATIENT PATIENT.
White bread; GHOST TOAST.
Wisecraker; FLIPS QUIPS.
Witch doctor; SINISTER MINISTER.
Witch doctor's mistake; VOODO BOO-BOO.
Witch purse; HAG BAG.
Woman; TENDER GENDER.
Woman driver; FENDER BENDER.
Woman gossip; GAB BAG.
Yeast; FLOUR POWER.
Young coal digger; MINOR MINER.
Young female monarch; TEEN QUEEN.
Zoo keeper; CRITTER SITTER.

Rhyming Riddles

WHAT DO YOU CALL. . .
What do you call a baby with a fever?
  A hotsy totsy.
What do you call a bird who lives around cows?
  A dairy canary.
What do you call a bloody yarn?
  A gory story.
What do you call a conversation between dogs?
  A bow wow pow wow.
What do you call a convict's meal?
  A sinner dinner.
What do you call a crazy flower?
  A crazy daisy.
What do you call a cruel ruler?
  A mean queen.
What do you call a dill that keeps changing color?
  A fickle pickle.
Wht do you call a fake horse?
  A phony pony.
What do you call a fat rat?
  A flabby tabby.
What do you all a fine janitor?
  A super super.
What do you call a giant fish you get for half price?

A whale sale.
What do you call a fast tricycle?
A tot rod.
What do you call a 5¢ cucumber?
A nickel pickle.
What do you call a hobo who's been caught in the rain?
A damp tramp.
What do you call a kiss from a dog?
A pooch smooch.
What do you call a large shovel?
A bigger digger.
What do you call a man who likes to fool you?
A bluff buff.
What do you call a man who likes to tie knots?
A knot nut.
What do you call a man who washes whales?
A blubber scrubber.
What do you call a naked rabbit?
A bare hare.
What do you call a pharaoh who eats crackers in bed?
A crummy mummy.
What do you call a piece of chocolate dropped on the
beach?
A sandy candy.
What do you call a rodent who lives indoors?
A house mouse.
What do you call a rubber skeleton?
A phony boney.
What do you call a shy plaything?
A coy toy.
What do you call a small child who can't make up his
mind?
A maybe baby.
What do you call a wet seal?
A damp stamp.
What do you all a wet toad?
A soggy froggy.
What do you call a witch doctors's mistake?
A voodoo boo-boo.
What do you call an arithmetic trail?

A math path.

What do you call an insect that lives in a bottle?
  A jug bug.

What do you call an insect's car?
  A roach coach.

What do you all an overweight car?
  A heavy Chevy.

What do you call an overweight rodent?
  A fat rat.

What do you call breakfast food for spirits?
  Ghosties toasties.

What do you call something shot from a skinny bow?
  A narrow arrow.

What do you call wages paid to a food taster?
  A calorie salary.

What are you giving your mouth when you top talking?
  A yap nap.

What did Goldilocks break?
  The bears chairs.

What did Harold do on Christmas Eve?
  Harold caroled.

What did the butcher say to the delivery boy?
  Deliver the liver.

What did the fisherman get?
  A wet net.

What did the jeweler do?
  Sold gold.

What did we have when the haunted house burned down?
  Roast ghost.

What do black trees have?
  A dark bark.

What do rabbits use to pay for things they buy?
  Bunny money.

What do sheep use to tell time?
  A flock clock.

What do kids sell in summer?
  Homemade lemonade.

What do you get from a friendly bug?
  A bug hug.

What do you get when Southern crops go bad?

Rotten cotton.

What do you get when you drop your toast into tomato soup?
Red bread.

What do you get when you touch a live wire?
A volt jolt.

What do you hve if you eat ice cream on Monday?
A Monday sundae.

What do you have when they serve beer on a train?
A bar car.

What do you need if you hit your head getting out of bed?
More bedroom headroom.

What do you play in an air-conditioned poolroom?
Cool pool.

What do young sheep like on their toast?
Lamb jam.

What does a beekeeper live on?
Honey money.

What does a cleaner do?
He presses dresses.

What is a prisoner's last meal called?
A sinner dinner.

What is a public conveyance everybody is happy with?
A jolly trolley.

What is another name for thunderhead?
A loud cloud.

What is on the stove you shouldn't touch?
A hot pot.

What kind of arthemtic do you get in the tub?
Bath math.

What kind of tales do little monster like?
A gory story.

What should one boxer never give another boxer?
A low blow.

What should you buy if you like waffles?
A waffle raffle.

What will an excited waiter give you?
Nervous service.

Why did Noah object to the letter D?
Because it made the ark dark.

How did Sir Lancelot see in the dark?
  By Knight light.
If four couples went to a buffet, how many people dined?
  Eight ate.
Why is the letter W the most unfriendly letter?
  Because it makes ill will.

Unknown Abbreviations

ABBREVIATION: A word that is not an abbreviation.
ABBREV:
The abbreviation of abbreviation.

ABC:
A baby cot.
A baby cries.
A bad clue.
A bald customer.
A ballroom crowed.
A band concert.
A bank crisis.
A barn clock.
A bashful couple.
A baseball coach
A bathing cap.
A bathroom closet.
A bawdy cartoon.
A beach concert.
A bear collar.
A beer can.
A bent coin.
A better circus.
A big car.
A big conference.

A big crash.
A bigger check.
A bingo card.
A bird cage.
A birthday comic.
A bitter cake.
A bland cheese.
A blank card.
A bleeding cut.
A blessed change.
A blonde cutie.
A blood clot.
A blue coat.
A body count.
A boiled carp.
A bonded contract.
A book cover.
A boring clown.
A boucing check.
A boxing contest.
A bran cereal.
A brave cowboy.

A breakfast coffee.
A brilliant close-out.
A broiled cheeseburger.
A broken comb.
A brown cat.
A bublegum counter.
A business conference.
A burned candle.
A busted case.
A busy cop.
A butter cookie.
A button convention.
A buzzing camel.
A buying costumer.
Ability, breaks, courage.
Always be calm.
Always be careful.
Always be consistent.
Always be courteous.
Always bring cash.
Always bring children.
Always bring cookies.
Always buy candy.
Always buy carefully.
American born Chinese.
Avoid boring conversations.
AFA:
  Ask for advice.
AFAR:
  Ask for another raise.
AMOK:
  Am O.K.
ATT:
  Always try twice.
  A torn transcription.
AT&T:
  Always talking & talking.
AWOL:
  A wolf on leave.
  After women or ladies.
AYA:
  As you are.
BAB:

Bed and Board.
Bed and Breakfast.
BAD:
  Break a date.
BAG:
  Boys and girls.
BAR:
  Beat a retreat.
BAT:
  Bait a trap.
BBC:
  Better bring children.
  Big beer can.
  Big boy crying.
  Bring back car.
  Brown Bag Company.
  Buy better clothing.
  Buy big candies.
BC:
  Be calm.
  Before calories.
  Before color.
  Bring cash.
  Bring children.
  Birth control.
BLBRMTH:
  Abbreviation for
    "Blabbermouth."
BIN:
  Believe it now.
BOAC:
  Bring over American cash.
BOW:
  Ball of wax.
BTW:
  By the way.
  By the week.
BUG:
  Brooklyn Union Gas.
BYOB:
  Bring your own bottle.
CAR:
  Can anyone race?

231

Can anyone run?
CBS:
Call big sister.
Call both sides.
Cash brings success.
Children be seated.
Children be silent.
Coffee be served.
Come Back Someday.
Come back soon.
Come before supper.
Come buy something.
Constantly Busy, Sir!
Creamed bacon sandwich.
CIA:
Call in anytime.
Can I apply?
Carry it all.
Cash in accepted.
Cash in advance.
Caught in action.
Come in again.
Come in anyhow.
Come in anytime.
Culinary Institute of
America.
Cut it apart.
CIO:
Change it over.
Check if off.
Check it out.
Clean it off.
Clip it on.
Count it out.
Cross it over.
Cross it out.
Cut it open.
Cut it out.
Cut it off.
COD:
Call old daddy.
Call on daddy.
Came over drunk.

Charge old daddy.
Cop on duty.
Crushed on delivery.
COLA:
Cost of living adjustment.
COP:
Call on people.
Capture old people.
Come over promptly.
Collect oldd papers.
Constable on patrol.
Copy on paper.
Cut out pictures.
COW:
Come over Wednesday.
Congress of Women.
Cut out waste.
CPA:
Car parking attendant.
Card Printing Agency.
Certified public alcoholic.
DA:
Don't ask.
Day after day.
DAD:
Dime a dozen.
DADDY:
Did anyone do dishes yet?
DAILY:
Daddy and I love you.
DAO:
Do as ordered.
DC:
Damn crowded.
Defective car.
Direct current.
Dirty children.
Divorce City.
Divorce court.
Don't call.
Don't cash.
Don't come.
Don't cough.

Don't coy.
Don't cry.
Double count.
Drive carefully.
Dumb children.
Duplicate copy.
DDT:
Dead drunk today.
Dear don't touch.
Diplomatic double-talk.
Direct dail telephone.
Disco dancing tonight.
Do dirty tricks.
Doesn't Do Tricks.
Don't do tricks.
Don't drink tea.
DEAR:
Drop everything and read.
DELTA:
Don't ever let them answer.
DIET:
Dare I Eat That?
DIN:
Destroy it now.
Divide it now.
Do it next.
Do it now.
DJ:
Don't jaywalk.
Don't joke.
DND:
Do not disturb.
DOA:
Drunk on arrival.
DR:
Dinning room.
Don't run.
ESP:
Especially stupid people.
Extra spending power.
Extra sensitive people.
FAD:
For a day.

FAQ:
Frequently asked questions.
FBI:
Fabulous buiness interests.
Fat, Bold, Ignorant.
Father butts in.
Female body inspector.
Fire burning intensily.
Five brothers interested.
Foes being investigated.
Food being investigated.
Fools breed ignorance.
For better information.
For bigger intermissions.
Forever being ignorant.
Forever being insulted.
FBI:
Foul ball inside.
Free beer inside.
Fuller Brush Incorporated.
Funny but insulting.
Fidelity, Bravery, Integrity.
FM:
Fine mother.
For me?
F2F:
Face to face.
FUBBS:
Fouled up beyond belief.
GAP:
Get a paper.
Get a permit.
Get a pet.
GAP:
Go away plese!
GI:
General industry.
Go instantly.
Great idea.
Gross income.
GM:
General manager.
Get mother.

Gone mad.
Good match.
Good morning.
Good motor.
Grand mother.
Great man.
Great meal.
GOK:
Good only knows.
HAH:
Have a heart.
HAND:
Have a nice day.
HAY:
How are you?
HP:
Hot potato.
HUMOR:
Help us maintain our
reason!
IBM:
I Bring Money.
I buy more.
Invite better men.
Is better made.
Is big money.
I've been misled.
IDK:
I don't know.
ITTT:
It takes two to tango.
ILLI:
I love Long Island.
INC:
I need cash.
IQ:
I quaff.
I qualify.
I quash.
I quench.
I quilty.
I quip.
I quirt.

I quit.
I quite.
I quote.
IRS:
I'm really sorry.
I'm really suffering.
I resume speeding.
I return shortly.
Internation Railroad
Station.
KISS:
Keep it simple, stupid!
KOCH:
Keep our children happy!
KP:
Keep leeling.
LI-LI-LI:
Long Island Lifetime
INcome.
Loan Insurance.
LOL:
Laughing out loud.
LSD:
Last single dollar.
Lox, salami & doughnut.
LX:
Large eggs.
MC:
Master Card.
Meat counter.
Mental case.
Merry Christmas.
My car.
MD:
Mail delivery.
Male doctor.
Man drinking.
Many disaster.
May Day.
Me doctor!
Mentally deficient!
Minimum deficit.
Minor damage.

Modern design.
Money deducted.
Money due.
More dough.
Mother's do!
Motor damaged.
My daddy!
My date.
My doctor.
My doughnut.
My dream.
My drink.
My dress.
Mutual document.

M.G.M.:
Makes Good Movies.
My Grand Mother.

MOB:
Man over board!

MOO:
Must obey orders!

MP:
My parents.
Missing person.
Monthly payments.
More pay.

NBC:
Never bring candy.
Never bring children.
Never borrow clothes.
New bread crumbs.
New broad cast.
New business closing.
Nine big cows.
No-body came!
No-body cares!
Nobody brought candies.
Nothing but cash.
Now bring cash!
Now buy clothes.

NEWS:
Need energic water savers.
North, East, West, South.

NIP:
Not important person.

NY:
Never yawn.
New York.

MYU:
New York unemployment.

OOB:
Out of business.

OOD:
Out of danger.

OOC:
Out of cash.

OOL:
Out of luck.

OOS:
Out of space.

OSS:
Older sister spying.

OOT:
Out of turn.

OTOH:
On the other hand.

OUP:
Out of practice.
Out of paper.
Out of patient.

PAN:
Pick a number.

PCA:
Please come again!

PD:
Pay doctor.
Police Department.
Postage due!

PhD:
Pay half dollar.
Pay hight duty.
Paid hundred dollars.
Pretty heavy date.

PIN:
Pay it now.
Pick it now.

Place it now.
Prove it now.
PIT:
Press it together.
PM:
Paid merchandise.
Paste mixer.
Pay master.
Pay me.
Post Master.
Power machine.
Prime meat.
Prime minister.
Pay more.
POB:
Pay old bills.
POP:
Piece of paper.
POW:
Play on words.
PS:
Pay soon.
Pay steward.
Pay super.
Pea soup.
Personal service.
Plane steward.
Play safe!
Please, silent!
Please sing.
Please sstop.
Police station.
Post script.
Poster sale.
Private school.
Private secretary.
Private sector.
Public school.
Pup sale.
PTA:
Pa tried again.
Parents tell all.
Parents threatening action.

Parents tip-toeing away.
Principal taking aspirin.
PTO:
Please take over.
Plese turn over.
PTP:
Pay the piper.
Person to person.
Pick to pieces.
Pull the plug.
Pound the pavement.
PUN:
Play upon names.
RDA:
Rich dessert assessment.
Related digestive
abnormality.
Recommended dietery
allowance;
RSVP:
Refreshment served very
promptly!
Remember sending
vedding presents.
Rush-in, shake hands,
vanish promptly.
Sin:
Stop it now!
SIR:
Set it right.
Son is returning.
Son is running.
Soon I run.
Sun is rising.
SIS:
Stay in school.
SNAFU:
Situation now all fouled up!
SOB:
Same old buddies.
Selling old beer.
Senate Office Building.
Son of Boss.

SOS:
  Same old shoes.
  Same old speech.
  Same old story.
  Same old stuff.
  Same, only softer.
  Same overcooked
    spaghetti.
  Save our ship.
  Save our souls.
  See other side.
  Send over sea.
  Share our supper.
  Shine our shoes.
  Sing our song.
  Smell our smog.
  Son operating shaver.
  Stamp out school.
  Stamp our Stamps.
  Steak or spaghetti?
  Stop on signal.
  Stop on street.
  Suspend other services.
  Swim or sink!

STOP:
  Save the old party!

SUR:
  As you are.

TAP:
  Take a part.
  Take a picture.
  Take a pill.
  Take a powder.
  Taxes are paid.
  Turn a page.

TFT:
  Tea for two.
  Table for two.

TGIF:
  Thanks God it's Friday!
  Toes Go In First.

TIE:
  Take it easy.

TIP:
  To insure promptness!

TNT:
  Take night train.
  Try no tricks.

TOT:
  Teller of tales.

TV:
  Terrible value.
  Total vacuum.

TWA:
  Talk with another.
  To walk alone.
  Travel with aunt.
  Try walking away.

UFO:
  Unnecessary food order.
  Unpaid fur overcoat.

UN:
  Unwanted neighbors.

VD:
  Vitamin efficiency.

VIB:
  Very insisting bore.

VIP:
  Very important person.
  Very impossible person.

WAR:
  We are ready!

WASP:
  We alwlays say please.

WAY:
  We admire you!

WCTU:
  Whiskey can't touch us!

WEST:
  Will everybody stop talking?

WHY:
  We hate you!

WIN:
  Walk in nude.

WIT:
  Wisdom in titbits.

237

WNBC:
    We never buy candy!
    We never bring children!
WYS:
    Watch your step.
X:
    Eggs.
YMCA:
    You may come anytime!
    You must come alone!
ZIP:
    Zoning improvement plan.

More Abbreviations

The same letters;

AAA: Automatic Awning Association,

BBB: Beautiful Bridal Boutique.
Better buy butter.
Brown baked beans.
Buy had blocks.
Buy better bargains.
Buy better books.
Buy better butter.
Buy bigger bargains.
Buy bigger bulbs.

BBBB: Buy better baseball bats.

BBBBB:
Better buy bigger Bond bread,

CCC: Certified coin collector.
Colossal civic center.
Cookies, cake, candies.
County Criminal Court.
Crossbun Cookies Company.

CCCC: Cheap chocolate chip-cookies.
Cut Christmas cake carefully.

DDD: Dinner dance date.

239

	Don't drive drunk.
	Drink-drive-die!
EEE:	Everybody eats eggs,
FFF:	Find fresh flowers.
	Fine fake furs.
	Fine fresh fish.
	Fine fur factory.
	Form fitting furcoats.
	Fresh fish fillet.
FFFF:	Fine firm-form farm,
FFFFFFFF:	Former farmer forms firm frame for fresh fish,
GGG:	Get great gifts.
	Great Goose Grocery,
HHH:	Happy Heart Huntinglodge.
	Have happy holidays.
	Hazy-hot-humid,
III:	International Insurance Inc.
LLL:	Live! Love! Laugh!
	Long lasting love.
	Lovely linen laundry,
MMM:	Meeting-mating-marriage.
	Make mine milk.
	Make min mink.
	Make more money,
NN:	Neither nor,
OOO:	On our own.
	One of ours.
	One onion only.
	Only one orange.
	Order only omelettes.
	Our own oven.
	Out of order.
PPP:	Perfect paper products.
	Perfect pecan pizza.
	Permanent parking permit.
	Please pay promptly,
RRR:	Relieved-recorded-relayed.
	Restful recreation restaurant,
SSS:	Sate security shutters.

	Shrimp salad sandwish.
	Super sardine sale.
	Sure sharp scissors.
	Sure snow skilodge,
TTT:	Tall tale tellers,
TTTT:	Timely tax tip topic,
TTT-TTT:	Try to tip through the tulips twice,
UUUU:	United underground union underwear,
WW:	Why wait?
WWW:	We will wait.
	We will walk.
	We wish windows.
	White western wine.
	Window washers worshop,
WWWW:	We won't waste water!
WWW-WWW:	We will wash without water willingly!
WWWW-WWW:	We, white Washington women, will wash woolen willingly.
WWWWW: WWWWW:	We will welcome wild women with warm watery worthless wine.

Many times a whole sentence can
be made up with abbreviations;
like; Many a man with a B.A. M.A.
and PhD had no JOB. I gave you a
IOU to UPS for a COD, from A&S
and G.E.